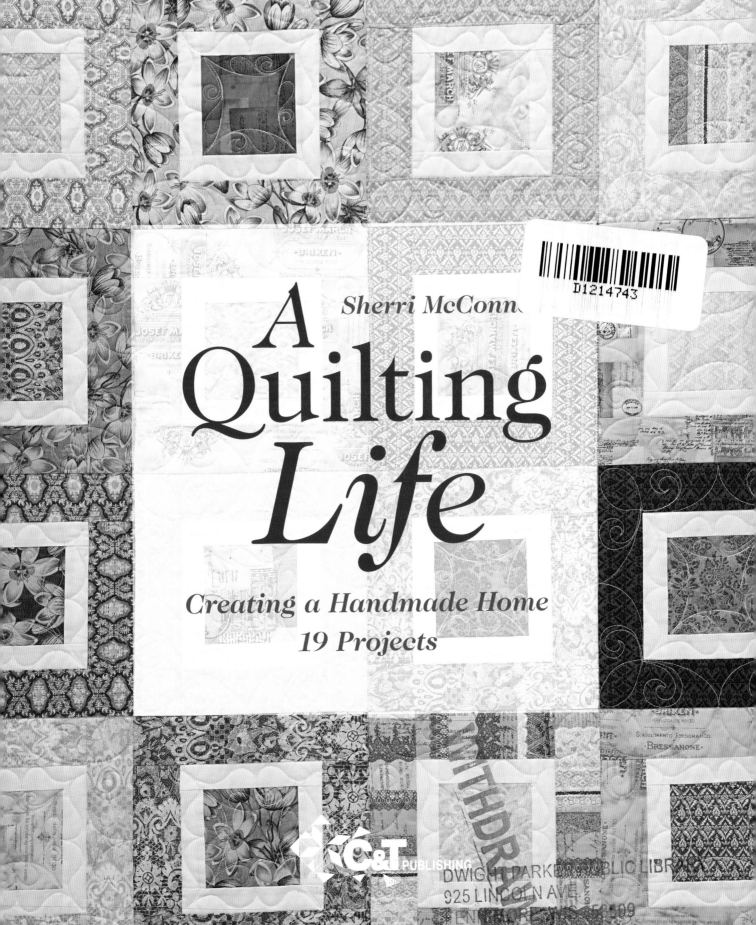

Sherri McConnell

A Quilting Life

Creating a Handmade Home

19 Projects

C&T PUBLISHING

Publisher: Amy Marson

Creative Director: Gailen Runge

Art Director: Kristy Zacharias

Editor: Lynn Koolish

Technical Editors: Ellen Pahl and Gailen Runge

Cover/Book Designer: April Mostek

Production Coordinator: Jenny Davis

Production Editor: Alice Mace Nakanishi

Illustrator: Valyrie Friedman

Photo Assistant: Cara Pardo

Photography by Christina Carty-Francis and Diane Pedersen of C&T Publishing, Inc., unless otherwise noted

Published by C&T Publishing, Inc., P.O. Box 1456, Lafayette, CA 94549

Library of Congress Cataloging-in-Publication Data

McConnell, Sherri, 1966-

  A quilting life : creating a handmade home - 19 projects / Sherri McConnell.

    pages cm

  ISBN 978-1-60705-659-1 (soft cover)

1. Patchwork--Patterns. 2. Quilting--Patterns. 3. Interior decoration. I. Title.

TT835.M399615 2013

746.46--dc23

2012031513

Printed in China

10 9 8 7 6 5 4 3 2

Contents

Dedication

To my wonderful husband, Bill, and my amazing children, Billy, Candace, Chelsi, and Sean, who have accepted the fact that there is always thread on my clothing and that fabric often lives at the end of the dining table while we are eating Sunday dinner. They have put up with my late-night sewing and fabric obsession for years. Thank you from the bottom of my heart.

And to my maternal grandmother, Jean Bice Bontrager Wilkins, whose lifelong journey of creating and quiltmaking has inspired me since childhood. Thank you, Grandma, for answering my question about why you would cut up beautiful fabrics into little pieces just to sew them back together, by teaching me to quilt.

Acknowledgments

To the following people, I appreciate more than words can say your support, inspiration, and friendship:

- Lissa Alexander, who provided words of encouragement before we had even met in "real life." Thank you (and Moda fabrics) for providing so much of the fabric that made this book possible.

- Camille Roskelley, Carrie Nelson, and Joanna Figueroa for teaching and inspiring me through your beautiful designs (and for answering my endless questions). Thanks to the three of you for also providing last-minute fabric!

- Andrea Marquez of the Christmas Goose in Las Vegas, Nevada. My first block of the month came from her shop, and she has beautifully quilted so many of my favorite quilts for many years.

- Judi Madsen and Gail Begay for working their longarm quilting magic with so many of my quilts and projects … and many times on short notice.

- Korindi Olson Totten for taking such amazing photographs—I love your photography!

- My blog readers, who provide so much encouragement, and all of the other quilting bloggers who share their ideas and inspiration on a daily basis.

- Susanne Woods, Lynn Koolish, Ellen Pahl, April Mostek, Jenny Davis, Alice Mace Nakanishi, and all of the people at C&T Publishing who made this book a reality.

- And finally, thanks so much, Mom, for giving me my own sewing machine when I was ten, for encouraging me to sew and create, and for always believing I could achieve any goal I set.

Introduction

A Quilting Life. This was the first title I thought of when starting my blog and the first title that came to mind when beginning the journey of creating this book. I've always quilted to create beautiful things for my home and for the people I love, and that's what a quilting life is all about.

From the beginning of my journey in writing this book, I've had a clear idea of some of the things I wanted to include. Practical tips and ideas were a must-have on the list, and providing projects that would appeal to today's quilter was another requirement. Since I love finishing and being able to use the things I create, I've included projects in this book that aren't too time-consuming. If you need a quick gift, a pillow or table runner can usually be created in an afternoon or day. Want to freshen up your decor for an upcoming holiday or event? Again, pillows and runners often fit the bill. In addition, the quilts I've designed for this book are beginner and intermediate projects—projects that will enable you to finish a quilt fast when you want to use it now.

A Quiltmaking Heritage

Sewing machine and quilt of Virginia Lee Fitzgarrald Bice (my maternal great-grandmother)

In the beginning … I was not going to be a quilter. It wasn't that I didn't come from a family of women who sewed and stitched over several generations. It wasn't that I didn't love to sew. I had sewn pretty much everything from clothing to curtains and even did quite a bit of needlework, but I just didn't "get" quiltmaking. My grandmother began making quilts after many years of sewing, crochet, and crafts, and pretty soon quiltmaking was her main creative outlet. She joined a local guild and began entering quilts in local shows. Before long she was bringing home ribbons to share with the family. Her traditional handmade gifts for birthdays and Christmas became quilted presents. I still remember the day I asked her why she spent so much time cutting up beautiful fabrics just to sew them back together. I remember also that she smiled and didn't seem to take any offense at my question.

A few years after my "why do you quilt" discussion, my oldest child was in need of a comforter for his bed. Since my grandmother had made baby quilts for each of my children, I asked her to make a twin-size quilt for her oldest grandson. Wisely, she told me no but offered to buy the fabric for the quilt and show me how to make it myself.

Grandma insisted I use the Double Irish Chain Quilt-in-a-Day pattern published by Eleanor Burns, and we made a trip to the local quilt shop to purchase fabrics and batting for the quilt. I spent just one day sewing with my grandmother, and then she went home, leaving me to finish the quilt on my own. That was all it took—and the rest, as they say, was (well, in my case) a quiltmaking obsession. For quite a while I seemed destined to make only double Irish chain quilts for the rest of my life; I made one for each of my daughters and made baby-sized versions of the quilt to give as gifts to friends who were expecting. When I found out I was going to have another child, I immediately made a baby double Irish chain for him! I don't know how many quilts I made using that pattern, but there were many.

After a couple of years I started making quilted pillows and wallhangings like my grandmother made. I was a little hesitant to try new patterns, but joining a block-of-the-month program through a local quilt shop changed everything. Even though I was still not very accomplished as a quilter, I had the courage to keep trying new things. And then I discovered quiltmaking blogs; this opened up a whole new world of inspiration and being able to learn from and share with others.

As I began calling myself a quilter, I wanted to know more about my family's quiltmaking heritage. I knew my grandmother had some family quilts. I longed to know the history of these quilts and to know more about my great-great-grandmothers, who had created them. I asked my grandmother and her two living sisters (one of her sisters had passed away before I began my project) to write their memories of quiltmaking in our family. Each history I received is a treasure to me. I wish I could include every anecdote here that I learned from their priceless letters.

My grandmother's earliest quilting-related memories were of visiting her Fitzgarrald grandparents as a very young girl. Her grandmother (my great-great-grandmother) would have the neighborhood ladies over to quilt. The women had lunch in the dining room and then assembled in the parlor to begin hand quilting a quilt that had been set up on a quilting frame. My grandmother was allowed to play under the frame while they sewed. This was in about 1926 or 1927.

According to family recollection, my great-great-grandmother Emma Acelia Wakefield Fitzgarrald was given a sewing machine from her father when she was a young girl. A sewing machine salesman had come to their door and had Emma demonstrate the machine for the family. Her father decided to purchase the machine and said, "Emma, now that you have a sewing machine, you can sew for yourself and all of your brothers." Emma had six brothers and spent a lot of time sewing, as you can imagine.

When she became a wife and busy mother, Emma Fitzgarrald usually received new fabric for quilts each week. Grandpa Fitzgarrald would hitch the horse and buggy and head into town (Center Point, Iowa) with the week's accumulation of eggs to sell. He bought groceries with the money from the eggs and often stopped by the dry goods store, where he chose a length of fabric to take home to his wife. He purchased enough for her to make a dress and apron, with plenty left over for quilt-making. The Bear's Paw quilt (shown rolled up below) contains fabrics that my grandmother remembers seeing in the dresses and aprons her grandmother wore. Emma Fitzgarrald lived with my grandmother for the last couple of years of her life and taught my grandmother to appliqué while she was living there.

Bear's Paw quilt, pieced by Emma Acelia Wakefield Fitzgarrald

Dresden quilt: Blocks made by Emma Acelia Wakefield Fitzgarrald before 1936 and assembled and quilted by her granddaughter Jean Lee Ella Bice Bontrager Wilkins.

Lily quilt: Appliquéd and quilted by Mary Gilchrist Bice for her granddaughter, my grandmother. My grandmother chose this pattern and these fabrics when she was a teenager. Then, the quilt was given to her upon her wedding.

When Grandma Fitzgarrald passed away, she left a stack of Dresden quilt blocks that were divided between my grandmother and her sisters. Many years passed before my grandmother did anything with these blocks, but in the 1980s she set the blocks into the quilt that is now a treasured heirloom that has been passed down from one generation to the next.

I have a few of those Dresden blocks in my possession today. One hangs on the design wall in my sewing room where I am able to look at it each day. A couple of other blocks I made into pillows to remind me of my wonderful quiltmaking heritage.

My grandmother's paternal grandmother, Mary Gilchrist Bice, was also a quilter who made many quilts for family members. When my grandmother was a teenager, her grandma Bice asked her to choose a pattern for a quilt. My grandmother chose a beautiful lily appliqué pattern in the colors of red, green, and white. On February 11, 1939, Mary Gilchrist Bice recorded in her journal: "Finished appliquéing the lily quilt today. Was 6 weeks in making it."

I am truly grateful for this quiltmaking heritage, and even more grateful that I was able to collect the bits and pieces of the stories that make our family quilts come to life. It's so important to have a record of one's quiltmaking history. Even if you are the first person in your family to embrace this amazing art, I strongly encourage you to record the path that led you to become a quilter!

Pillows

Patchwork pillows have long been one of my favorite items to make for my home and to give to others as gifts. In fact, my first machine-sewing project was a set of two patchwork pillows made from precut squares my mom had purchased at the fabric store. Pillows are the perfect way to try out a new technique or practice a block for a larger quilt—almost any size block can be made into a fun pillow.

The pillows in this chapter were made and designed to showcase the fabrics and to add character to the places where they sit. The Little Hexagon Flower Pillow (page 10) was made for my sewing room. Our living room has solid gray sofas, and making the pillows using the Amy Butler fabrics (pages 17, 19, and 21) adds just the right amount of color and pop to the room. The Christmas Dresden Pillow (page 13) stays in the living room on a chair during the holidays.

Pieced and quilted by Sherri McConnell
Fabric collection: Flea Market Fancy by Denyse Schmidt

Little Hexagon Flower Pillow

Finished block: 6½″ × 6½″ • *Finished pillow:* 12″ × 12″

I'm absolutely drawn to the simple charm of hexagon flowers! I love them made with matching petals and a coordinating center, and I also love them scrappy. This project goes together quickly and "plants" a simple flower wherever it's placed. The pillow is small enough to fit in many places and yet large enough to make an impact.

Fabrics

Assorted prints:* 11 squares approximately 4″ × 4″ and 4 scraps at least 2″ × 12″

White: ⅓ yard

Pillow back: ½ yard

Binding: ¼ yard

Batting: 14″ × 14″

Muslin: 14″ × 14″

* You can use a Charm Pack for the hexagons and corner triangle pieces if desired.

Notions

1″ hexagon templates:** 7

Pillow form: 12″ × 12″

** I use premade hexagon templates from www.paperpieces.com. You can also make your own from freezer paper as instructed in Block Assembly (at right).

Cutting

Assorted print fabrics:
- Cut 4 squares 2″ × 2″ for corner triangles.
- Cut 2 strips 2″ × 9″ for outer side borders.
- Cut 2 strips 2″ × 12″ for outer top and bottom borders.

White fabric:
- Cut 1 square 9″ × 9″ for block background.
- Cut 2 strips 1½″ × 7″ for inner side borders.
- Cut 2 strips 1½″ × 9″ for inner top and bottom borders.

Pillow back fabric:
- Cut 1 square 12″ × 12″ and 1 rectangle 12″ × 10″.

Binding fabric:
- Cut 2 strips 2¼″ × width of fabric.

Block Assembly

Refer to The Basics (pages 70–77) as needed. Seam allowances are ¼″ unless otherwise noted.

1. Cut 7 fabric hexagons using one of the following methods:

Freezer paper Using the pattern (page 12), trace 7 hexagons onto the dull side of freezer paper using a fine-point Sharpie marker or other permanent pen. Cut them out ½″ beyond the drawn lines. Iron the shiny side of the freezer-paper templates to the dull side of another piece of freezer paper; cut the template out along the drawn line. Press the shiny side of the 2-layer template to the wrong side of the 4″ fabric squares. Cut out the fabric ⅜″ beyond the edge of the template.

Purchased or cardstock templates Place the template on the wrong side of the fabric and cut it out ⅜″ beyond the edge of the template. You can secure the paper template to the fabric with a plastic-coated paper clip while basting.

2. Baste the hexagons by folding the sides down at each corner and taking a small slipstitch through the fabric on the wrong side of the hexagon piece. Continue all the way around the hexagon, stitching through only the fabric, and tie off the thread with a knot.

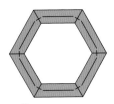

Baste at corners.

3. To make the hexagon flower, place the center hexagon and one of the outer petals right sides together, aligning the edges. Whipstitch the 2 hexagons together along one edge from the wrong side. Continue using the whipstitch to attach each hexagon in a similar manner until you have a completed flower.

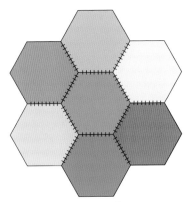

Make hexagon flower.

About the Pillows

I've included instructions for making flap-opening backs on all of the pillows. With these openings, you can easily insert and remove a pillow form. If you like, sew a snap to the flaps to secure the opening.

The measurements given result in pillow backs that are the same size as the pillow fronts. Some people like to initially make their pillow backs larger on all sides and then trim the back to match the front after the back and front have been sewn together. If you would like to do this just add 1″ to all pillow back measurements.

4. Carefully remove the paper from the basted flower and press the hexagon flower well using spray starch.

5. Center the hexagon flower on the 9″ × 9″ white background square. Secure the hexagon flower to the background with small pins or appliqué glue (see Appliqué Basics, pages 74 and 75). Appliqué the flower to the background fabric.

6. Press the appliquéd piece carefully on the wrong side and trim the background to 7″ × 7″, keeping the hexagon flower centered.

7. Using the Corner-Square Triangles technique (page 74), draw a diagonal line from corner to corner on the wrong side of the 2″ squares. Place a marked square right side down on the corner of the 7″ background square, line up the edges, sew on the drawn line, and trim. Repeat for each corner.

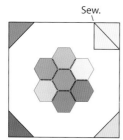
Sew.

Add corner triangles.

8. Sew the 1½″ × 7″ white border strips to the left and right sides of the hexagon flower block. Press the seams toward the borders. Sew the 1½″ × 9″ white border strips to the top and bottom of the hexagon flower block. Press the seams toward the borders.

9. Sew the 2″ × 9″ print strips to the left and right sides of the hexagon flower block. Press the seams toward the print borders. Sew the 2″ × 12″ print strips to the top and bottom of the hexagon flower block. Press the seams toward the print borders.

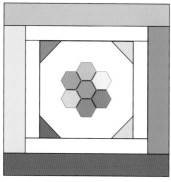
Pillow top assembly

Pillow Assembly

1. Place the 14″ × 14″ square of batting on top of the square of muslin. Center the pillow top on the batting, baste the layers together, and quilt as desired. I quilted by hand ⅛″ around the hexagon flower, ⅛″ on the inside of the hexagon flower block, ⅛″ on both sides of the inner border, and ¼″ in the outer border.

2. Trim the batting and muslin even with the edges of the pillow top.

3. Make the pillow back by folding in and pressing ¼″ on one 12″ edge of each pillow back rectangle. Fold again, press, and sew to create a finished edge.

4. Turn the hemmed edges under 2″, wrong sides of fabric together, and press.

5. Place the smaller pillow back rectangle on top of the completed pillow top, wrong sides together, and pin. Place the second pillow back rectangle on top of this unit and pin. The pillow back sections should overlap each other. Baste these sections with a scant ¼″ seam. The area in the back where the pillow back sections overlap will allow you to insert the pillow form into the pillow.

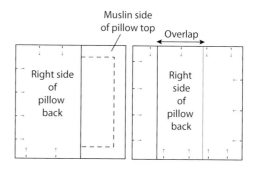
Muslin side of pillow top
Overlap
Right side of pillow back
Right side of pillow back

6. Bind the edges of the pillow (see Binding, pages 76 and 77).

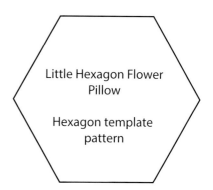
Little Hexagon Flower Pillow

Hexagon template pattern

Pieced and hand quilted by Sherri McConnell
This is a scrappy pillow—fabrics are from a variety of collections.

Christmas Dresden Pillow

Finished block: 10″ × 10″ • *Finished pillow:* 14″ × 14″

The Dresden Plate is another quilt pattern that just calls out to be made in a variety of fabrics. I love this scrappy version, made with a medley of modern Christmas prints. Choosing the fabric for the center circle is always my favorite part of making a Dresden!

13

Fabrics

Assorted prints and solids:* ¼ yard total

White: ½ yard

Border: ¼ yard

Pillow back: ½ yard

Binding: ¼ yard

Batting: 18″ × 18″

Muslin: 18″ × 18″

* Use as many different fabrics as you can to create a whimsical look. You can use a Charm Pack for the Dresden wedges and center circle if desired.

Notions

Pillow form: 14″ × 14″

Tool: Easy Dresden tool by Darlene Zimmerman (see Resources, page 78) or freezer paper

Cutting

If you don't have the Easy Dresden tool, make a template using freezer paper and the pattern (page 16), following the instructions in Making Freezer-Paper Templates (page 74). You'll also need to make a circle template in the same manner using the pattern (page 16). Another option for the center circle is to use premade Mylar templates from Karen Kay Buckley's Bigger Perfect Circles (see Resources, page 78).

Assorted print fabrics:
- Cut 20 Dresden wedges. If you are using the Easy Dresden tool, use the 3½″ mark as your guide.
- Cut 1 circle ¼″ larger than the circle template.

White fabric:
- Cut 1 square 12½″ × 12½″ for block background.

Border fabric:
- Cut 2 strips 2½″ × 10½″ for side borders.
- Cut 2 strips 2½″ × 14½″ for top and bottom borders.

Pillow back fabric:
- Cut 1 square 14½″ × 14½″ and 1 rectangle 12″ × 14½″.

Binding fabric:
- Cut 2 strips 2¼″ × width of fabric.

Block Assembly

Refer to The Basics (pages 70–77) as needed. Seam allowances are ¼″ unless otherwise noted.

1. Fold the Dresden wedges in half lengthwise, right sides together. Sew a ¼″ seam across the wide edge of the Dresden. Trim as necessary to eliminate bulk. Turn the point of the Dresden right side out, making a sharp point. Center the sewn seam and press.

Tip

When sewing the seam across the top of the Dresden wedge, be sure to backstitch at the folded edge. This will ensure that your seam does not come loose when turning the wedge right side out, helping you to have a wedge with a crisp, sharp point.

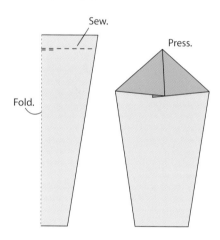

2. Join all 20 Dresden wedges by sewing ¼″ seams along the long edges of the wedges. Start the seam near the top edge of the wedges to ensure that the outside edges will line up.

Backstitch at the beginning of each seam. Press the seams in one direction.

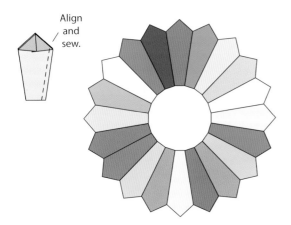

Align and sew.

3. Center the joined Dresden wedges on the block background. Pin it in place using small pins or appliqué glue and appliqué it to the background fabric (see Appliqué Basics, pages 74 and 75).

4. Make the center circle by centering the template onto the fabric and then pressing the circle fabric to the freezer-paper template. Spray some liquid starch into a small bowl and paint around the edges of the fabric using a small paintbrush dipped into the spray starch. Iron the edges around the template. Remove the freezer-paper template and press again. (If you are using Bigger Perfect Circles, follow the instructions on the package.)

5. Center and appliqué the circle to the quilt block, making sure the circle is centered on the Dresden plate.

6. Trim the block to 10½″ × 10½″, making sure that the Dresden appliqué is centered.

7. Sew the 2½″ × 10½″ border strips to the left and right sides of the block. Press the seams toward the borders. Sew the 2½″ × 14½″ border strips to the top and bottom of the block. Press the seams toward the borders.

Pillow top assembly

Seasonal Pillows

I make small decorative pillows according to the season and place them on a small shelf just inside our front door. I also use seasonal pillows and pillows made from some of my favorite fabrics on beds, sofas, and chairs throughout our home. With pillows, the possibilities are endless! Because many of my pillows are seasonal, I remove the pillow forms and store all the pillows flat. I keep those that can be used with the same size inserts together, thus reducing the number of inserts I need to purchase and making off-season pillows easier to store.

Pillow Assembly

1. Place the 18″ × 18″ square of batting on the muslin. Center the pillow top on the batting and quilt as desired. I quilted ⅛″ around the edges of the Dresden and ¼″ on both sides of the seams where the inner block meets the border fabrics.

2. Trim the batting and muslin even with the edges of the pillow.

3. Make the pillow back by folding in and pressing ¼″ on one 14½″ edge of each pillow back section. Fold again, press, and sew to create a finished edge.

4. Press the hemmed edges in 3″, with the wrong sides of the fabric together.

5. To complete the pillow, follow Pillow Assembly, Steps 5 and 6, of Little Hexagon Flower Pillow (page 12).

Christmas Dresden Pillow

Circle template pattern

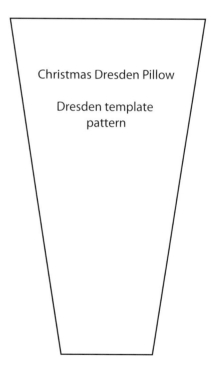

Christmas Dresden Pillow

Dresden template pattern

Pieced and quilted by Sherri McConnell
Fabric collections: Love by Amy Butler; Bella Solids by Moda

Mod Dresden Pillow

Finished block: 12½″ × 12½″ • *Finished pillow:* 17″ × 17″

I'm always fascinated by the way traditional quilt blocks and patterns just seem to come to life when paired with modern fabrics. A modern Dresden had been on my to-do list for quite some time when I made this one.

Fabrics

Assorted prints and solids:* ⅜ yard total

White: ½ yard

Border: ¼ yard

Pillow back: ⅝ yard

Binding: ¼ yard

Batting: 21″ × 21″

Muslin: 21″ × 21″

*You can use a Charm Pack for the Dresden wedges and center circle if desired.

Notions

Pillow form: 17″ × 17″

Tool: Easy Dresden tool by Darlene Zimmerman (see Resources, page 78) or freezer paper

Cutting

If you don't have the Easy Dresden tool, make a template using freezer paper and the pattern (below), following the instructions in Making Freezer-Paper Templates (page 74). You'll also need to make a circle template in the same manner using the pattern (below). Another option is to use premade Mylar templates from Karen Kay Buckley's Bigger Perfect Circles (see Resources, page 78).

Assorted print fabrics:
· Cut 20 Dresden wedges. If you are using the Easy Dresden tool, use the 5″ mark as your guide.
· Cut 1 circle ¼″ larger than the circle template.

White fabric:
· Cut 1 square 16″ × 16″ for block background.

Border fabric:
· Cut 2 strips 2½″ × 13″ for side borders.
· Cut 2 strips 2½″ × 17″ for top and bottom borders.

Pillow back fabric:
· Cut 1 square 17″ × 17″ and 1 rectangle 17″ × 14″.

Binding fabric:
· Cut 2 strips 2¼″ × width of fabric.

Mod Dresden Pillow

Dresden template pattern

Mod Dresden Pillow

Circle template pattern

Block Assembly

Refer to The Basics (pages 70–77) as needed. Seam allowances are ¼″ unless otherwise noted.

1. Follow Block Assembly, Steps 1–5, of Christmas Dresden Pillow (pages 14 and 15).

2. Trim the block to 13″ × 13″, making sure that the Dresden appliqué is centered.

3. Sew the 2½″ × 13″ border strips to the left and right sides of the block. Press the seams toward the borders. Sew the 2½″ × 17″ border strips to the top and bottom of the block. Press the seams toward the borders.

Pillow Assembly

1. Place the 21″ × 21″ square of batting on the muslin. Center the pillow top on the batting and quilt as desired. I hand quilted around the outside of the Dresden plate and also around the inside of the Dresden center circle.

2. Trim the batting and muslin even with the edges of the pillow top.

3. Make the pillow back by folding in and pressing ¼″ on one 17″ edge of each pillow back section. Fold again, press, and sew to create a finished edge.

4. Press the hemmed edges in 3″, with wrong sides of fabric together.

5. To complete the pillow, follow Pillow Assembly, Steps 5 and 6, of Little Hexagon Flower Pillow (page 12).

Pieced by Sherri McConnell and quilted by Gail Begay
Fabric collections: Love by Amy Butler; Bella Solids by Moda

Mod Pillow 1

Finished block: 3″ × 3″ • **Finished pillow:** 18″ × 18″

The mixture of solids and modern prints in this pillow showcases all of the
fabrics beautifully. I love the contrast between the solid white and solid gray,
and the use of the white for the pillow binding really sets everything off.

Fabrics

Assorted prints: ¼ yard total

White: ⅜ yard

Gray solid: ⅛ yard

Border: ¼ yard

Pillow back: ⅝ yard

Binding: ¼ yard

Batting: 22″ × 22″

Muslin: 22″ × 22″

Notions

Pillow form: 18″ × 18″

Cutting

Assorted print fabrics:
- Cut 5 squares 4½″ × 4½″ for Hourglass blocks.

White fabric:
- Cut 5 squares 4½″ × 4½″ for Hourglass blocks.
- Cut 2 strips 2″ × width of fabric; subcut into 2 strips 2″ × 11½″ and 2 strips 2″ × 14½″ for middle borders.

Gray fabric:
- Cut 2 strips 1½″ × width of fabric; subcut into 2 strips 1½″ × 9½″ and 2 strips 1½″ × 11½″ for inner borders.

Border fabric:
- Cut 2 strips 2½″ × width of fabric; subcut into 2 strips 2½″ × 14½″ and 2 strips 2½″ × 18½″ for outer borders.

Pillow back fabric:
- Cut 1 square 18½″ × 18½″ and 1 rectangle 18½″ × 16″.

Binding fabric:
- Cut 3 strips 2¼″ × width of fabric.

Block Assembly

Refer to The Basics (pages 70–77) as needed. Seam allowances are ¼″ unless otherwise noted.

1. Draw a diagonal line from corner to corner on the wrong side of the white 4½″ × 4½″ squares.

2. Place a white 4½″ × 4½″ square right sides together with a print 4½″ × 4½″ square and make half-square triangles. See Half-Square Triangles (page 73). Make 10.

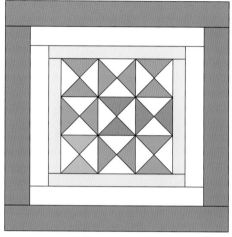

Make 10.

3. Draw a diagonal line from corner to corner perpendicular to the seam on the wrong side of one of the half-square triangle units. Place it right sides together with a matching half-square triangle unit, having the light and dark fabrics facing each other and nesting the seams together. Stitch a scant ¼″ on each side of the drawn line. Cut the squares apart on the drawn line and press the seam allowances to one side. You now have 2 Hourglass blocks. Trim each block to 3½″ × 3½″. Make 10. (You need 9; you'll have 1 extra.)

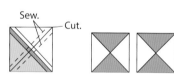

Sew.   Cut.

4. Choose 9 of the Hourglass blocks and arrange them into 3 rows of 3 blocks each. Rotate every other block 90° as shown in the pillow top assembly diagram. Sew the blocks into rows and press. Sew the rows together; press.

5. Sew the 1½″ × 9½″ gray inner border strips to the left and right sides of the pillow center. Press the seams toward the gray fabric. Sew the 1½″ × 11½″ gray inner border strips to the top and bottom. Press the seams toward the gray fabric.

6. Sew the 2″ × 11½″ white middle border strips to the left and right sides of the pillow top. Press the seams toward the white fabric. Sew the 2″ × 14½″ white middle border strips to the top and bottom. Press the seams toward the white fabric.

7. Sew the 2½″ × 14½″ print outer border strips to the left and right sides of the pillow top. Press the seams toward the border fabric. Sew the 2½″ × 18½″ print outer border strips to the top and bottom. Press the seams toward the border fabric.

Pillow top assembly

Pillow Assembly

1. Place the 22″ × 22″ square of batting on the muslin. Center the pillow top on the batting and quilt as desired. Gail machine quilted an allover feather pattern on the pillow top.

2. Trim the batting even with the edges of the pillow top.

3. Make the pillow back by folding in and pressing ¼″ on one 18½″ edge of each pillow back section. Fold again, press, and sew along the pressed edge to create a finished outside edge.

4. Press the hemmed edges in 2″, with wrong sides of the fabric together.

5. To complete the pillow, follow Pillow Assembly, Steps 5 and 6, of Little Hexagon Flower Pillow (page 12).

Pieced by Sherri McConnell and quilted by Gail Begay
Fabric collections: Love by Amy Butler; Bella Solids by Moda

Mod Pillow 2

Finished block: 5″ × 5″ • Finished pillow: 18″ × 18″

With this pillow I added a couple more solids while using the same
basic blocks used in Mod Pillow 1. The contrast is fun yet simple
and again gives classic, traditional blocks a modern twist.

Fabrics

Assorted prints and solids: ½ yard total

White: ⅜ yard

Pillow back: ⅝ yard

Binding: ¼ yard

Batting: 22″ × 22″

Muslin: 22″ × 22″

Notions

Pillow form: 18″ × 18″

Cutting

Assorted print and solid fabrics:

Note: Each block frame is made of 2 rectangles 1½″ × 3½″ and 2 rectangles 1½″ × 5½″ cut from the same fabric. The pillow shown has 4 different block frames.

- Cut 4 squares 4½″ × 4½″ for Hourglass blocks.
- Cut 1 square 3½″ × 3½″ for center block.
- Cut 1 matching set of 2 rectangles 1½″ × 3½″ and 2 rectangles 1½″ × 5½″ for center block frame.
- Cut 8 matching sets of 2 rectangles 1½″ × 3½″ and 2 rectangles 1½″ × 5½″ for Hourglass block frames.

White fabric:

- Cut 4 squares 4½″ × 4½″ for Hourglass blocks.
- Cut 2 strips 2″ × width of fabric; subcut into 2 strips 2″ × 15½″ and 2 strips 2″ × 18½″ for borders.

Pillow back fabric:

- Cut 1 square 18½″ × 18½″.
- Cut 1 rectangle 18½″ × 15½″.

Binding fabric:

- Cut 3 strips 2¼″ × width of fabric.

Block Assembly

Refer to The Basics (pages 70–77) as needed. Seam allowances are ¼″ unless otherwise noted.

1. Make 8 Hourglass blocks as described in Block Assembly, Steps 1–3, of Mod Pillow 1 (page 20).

2. Add frames to the 8 Hourglass blocks and the 3½″ × 3½″ print square by first sewing matching 1½″ × 3½″ rectangles to the left and right sides of each block. Press the seams toward the frames. Sew the 1½″ × 5½″ rectangles to the top and bottom of the blocks. Press the seams toward the frames.

3. Arrange the blocks into 3 rows of 3 blocks each. Sew the blocks together in each row and press the seams in opposite directions from row to row. Sew the rows together and press.

4. Sew the 2″ × 15½″ white border strips to the left and right sides of the pillow top. Press the seams toward the borders. Add the 2″ × 18½″ white border strips to the top and bottom of the pillow top. Press the seams toward the borders.

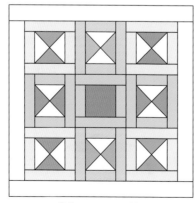

Pillow top assembly

Pillow Assembly

1. Place the 22″ × 22″ square of batting on the muslin. Center the pillow top on the batting and quilt as desired. Gail quilted an allover feather pattern on the pillow top.

2. Trim the batting and muslin even with the edges of the pillow top.

3. Make the pillow back by folding in and pressing ¼″ on one 18½″ edge of each pillow back rectangle. Fold again, press, and sew to create a finished edge.

4. Press the hemmed edges in 2″, with wrong sides of fabric together.

5. To complete the pillow, follow Pillow Assembly, Steps 5 and 6, of Little Hexagon Flower Pillow (page 12).

Handmade Gift Ideas

Small quilted projects make perfect handmade gifts. I love to give small pillows, table toppers, and runners as holiday and birthday gifts. Often you can use leftover blocks for these great gifts. Framed blocks, pot-holders, and placemats can also be made from leftover blocks and make easy quilted gifts.

Tabletop

Small quilts for tables and surfaces of all sizes are the perfect quick project to make for your home or to give as gifts. Most runner and topper patterns can be easily adapted to the perfect size for any piece of furniture: add or subtract blocks to make a longer or shorter runner for a table or dresser; set blocks from a runner pattern into a square for a table topper; or use just one block and add extra borders for a stunning centerpiece. Table runners and toppers can also be used as bed runners (with extra blocks added to have enough length) and as the perfect quilt for sofa backs and dresser tops.

Mod Runner

Finished block: 10″ × 10″
Finished runner: 14″ × 54″

This runner is one of those projects that was inspired by the fabrics. A table runner made with modern fabrics in a simple design can completely update any table setting. The mixture of solids and contemporary prints blends beautifully to give a vintage yet modern feel.

Pieced by Sherri McConnell
and quilted by Gail Begay
Fabric collections: Love by
Amy Butler; Bella Solids by Moda

Fabrics

Assorted prints and solids: ⅔ yard total

White:* ⅝ yard

Backing: 1¾ yards

Binding: ⅜ yard

Batting: 20˝ × 60˝

* If you prefer to cut the borders lengthwise, you'll need 1⅝ yards.

Cutting

Assorted print and solid fabrics:
- Cut 5 squares 4½˝ × 4½˝ for blocks.
- Cut 5 matching sets of 2 rectangles 2½˝ × 6½˝ and 2 rectangles 2½˝ × 10½˝ for block outer borders.

White fabric:
- Cut 3 strips 1½˝ × width of fabric; subcut into 10 rectangles 1½˝ × 4½˝ and 10 rectangles 1½˝ × 6½˝ for inner frames.
- Cut 2 strips 2½˝ × 10½˝ for border.
- Cut 3 strips 2½˝ × width of fabric for border.

Binding fabric:
- Cut 4 strips 2¼˝ × width of fabric.

Block Assembly

Refer to The Basics (pages 70–77) as needed. Seam allowances are ¼˝ unless otherwise noted.

1. Sew the 1½˝ × 4½˝ white rectangles to opposite sides of each of the 4½˝ × 4½˝ print squares. Press the seams toward the white fabric. Sew 1½˝ × 6½˝ white rectangles to the remaining sides. Press the seams toward the white fabric. Make 5.

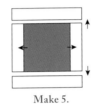

Make 5.

2. Sew matching 2½˝ × 6½˝ print or solid rectangles to opposite sides of a block unit from Step 1. Press the seams away from the block center. Sew the matching 2½˝ × 10½˝ print or solid rectangles to the remaining sides of the block unit. Press the seams away from the center. Repeat to make 5 blocks.

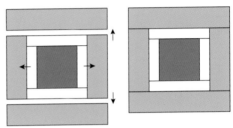

Block assembly

Runner Assembly

1. Arrange the blocks in a row as desired. Rotate every other block so that the block seams do not have to be matched. Stitch the blocks together and press.

2. Sew the 2½˝ × 10½˝ border strips to the short sides of the runner. Press the seams toward the borders.

3. Sew the three 2½˝ × 42˝ border strips together to make a long strip. Cut into 2 strips 2½˝ × 54½˝. Sew these to the long sides of the runner. Press the seams toward the borders.

4. Layer the backing, batting, and runner top. Quilt as desired. Bind the edges (see Binding, pages 76 and 77).

Runners for Dining Tables

For dining areas, I like to create runners that are fairly narrow so there is plenty of room for place settings on either side of the runner. The three runners in this chapter are all created with dining tables in mind; however, borders can easily be added to make the runners wider if you prefer.

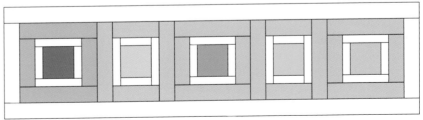

Runner assembly

Christmas Star Runner

Finished block: 12″ × 12″
Finished runner: 14″ × 66″

Nothing says Christmas like a star block made with a mix of fun fabrics! These blocks can also be made with traditional fabrics to create a completely different look. This is a quick project to make—perfect for gift giving at the holidays or anytime!

Pieced by Sherri McConnell and quilted by Gail Begay
Fabric collection: Jingle by Ann Kelle for Robert Kaufman

Fabrics

Assorted Christmas prints: 15 fat eighths or 15 rectangles 12˝ × 14˝

Background: ⅞ yard

Backing: 2⅛ yards

Binding: ½ yard

Batting: 20˝ × 72˝

Cutting

Note: For each star block, choose 3 different assorted prints; label them fabrics 1, 2, and 3.

5 assorted Christmas fabrics (fabric 1):
- Cut 1 square 4½˝ × 4½˝ *from each* for center squares.
- Cut 1 strip 2½˝ × 11˝ *from each* for corner squares.

5 assorted Christmas fabrics (fabric 2):
- Cut 4 rectangles 2½˝ × 4½˝ *from each* for star points.

5 assorted Christmas fabrics (fabric 3):
- Cut 4 rectangles 2½˝ × 4½˝ *from each* for star points.

Background fabric:
- Cut 8 strips 2½˝ × width of fabric; subcut into:

  5 strips 2½˝ × 11˝

  20 rectangles 2½˝ × 4½˝

  40 squares 2½˝ × 2½˝
- Cut 2 strips 1½˝ × width of fabric; subcut into:

  6 strips 1½˝ × 12½˝
- Cut 3 strips 1½˝ × width of fabric.

Binding fabric:
- Cut 5 strips 2¼˝ × width of fabric.

Block Assembly

Refer to The Basics (pages 70–77) as needed. Seam allowances are ¼˝ unless otherwise noted.

1. Sew a 2½˝ × 11˝ background strip to a 2½˝ × 11˝ strip of fabric 1. Press the seams toward the dark fabric. Cut the strip set into 4 pieces 2½˝ × 4½˝.

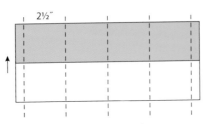

Sew strips together and cut.

2. Draw a diagonal line from corner to corner on the wrong side of each 2½˝ × 2½˝ background square.

3. Place a marked 2½˝ × 2½˝ background square right sides together with each of the 2½˝ × 4½˝ rectangles of fabrics 2 and 3. Sew the 2½˝ square to a fabric 2 strip along the marked line in one direction. Press the seams toward the background and trim the excess fabric. Sew a 2½˝ square to a fabric 3 strip in the opposite direction. Press the seams toward the print and trim the excess fabric. Repeat to make 4 of each unit for the block. (All the pieces from one fabric should be sewn in an identical manner, with the contrasting fabric sections sewn in a mirror image.)

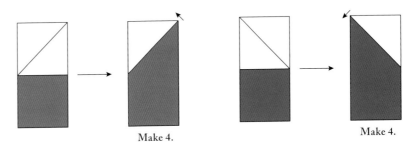

Make 4.   Make 4.

4. Sew a unit from Step 3 to a mirror-image unit to make a star point unit. Make 4.

Make 4.

Seasonal Table Toppers

By using holiday fabrics for runners and toppers, you can create the perfect home decor items and gifts. I love to switch table toppers and runners according to the season. When not in use, runners and toppers can be stored in dresser drawers, hung in closets, or rolled up and placed in baskets to decorate year-round. Larger quilts can also be turned on the diagonal and used as toppers for bigger tables.

Storing and Rotating Quilts

I love using quilts for decorating, and over the years I have come up with a few ways to help keep seasonal and other small quilts organized.

I keep a list of small quilts frequently used for decorating.

Quilts on this list are categorized by season or holiday. For each quilt I list where I store it when not in use and also list places in my home where I've used the quilt to decorate.

Recently I've added information that includes when the quilt was made and what fabric lines I used in its construction.

5. Assemble the block sections from Step 1 and Step 4 along with the 2½″ × 4½″ background rectangles and the 4½″ × 4½″ print squares as shown. Press. Repeat Steps 1–5 to make 5 blocks.

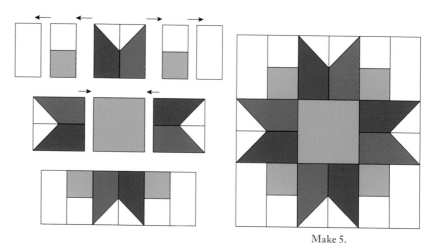

Make 5.

Runner Assembly

1. Arrange the 5 blocks in a row as desired. Sew the blocks together, alternating them with the 1½″ × 12½″ sashing strips, beginning and ending with sashing. Press the seams toward the sashing.

2. Sew the 1½″ × 40″ strips of background fabric together to make a long strip. Cut 2 strips 1½″ × 66½″ and sew them to the long edges of the runner center. Press the seams toward the strips.

3. Layer the backing, batting, and runner top. Quilt as desired. Bind the edges (see Binding, pages 76 and 77).

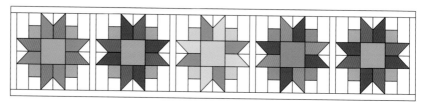

Runner assembly

Pieced by Sherri McConnell and quilted by Gail Begay
Fabric collection: American Banner Rose by Minick & Simpson for Moda

Hometown Summer Runner

Finished block: 12″ × 12″ • Finished runner: 20″ × 46″

Another favorite star block of mine creates a homey
summertime runner perfect for decorating all season long. These
stars would also be a lot of fun pieced together from the latest
florals and other new arrivals at your local quilt shop.

Fabrics

Assorted medium and dark prints: 6 fat eighths or 6 squares 10″ × 10″

Block background:* ⅜ yard or 3 fat eighths

Sashing and inner border: ¼ yard

Outer border: ½ yard

Backing: 1½ yards

Binding: ⅜ yard

Batting: 26″ × 52″

You can use one background fabric (⅜ yard) or a different one for each block (3 fat eighths).

Cutting

Assorted print fabrics (6):
· Cut 4 squares 4″ × 4″ *from each* for star blocks.

Background fabric:
· Cut 4 squares 4″ × 4″ and 4 squares 3½″ × 3½″ for each block (12 squares total of each size).

Sashing and inner border fabric:
· Cut 4 strips 1½″ × 12½″.
· Cut 2 strips 1½″ × 40½″.

Outer border fabric:
· Cut 2 strips 3½″ × 14½″.
· Cut 3 strips 3½″ × width of fabric.

Binding fabric:
· Cut 4 strips 2¼″ × width of fabric.

Block Assembly

Refer to The Basics (pages 70–77) as needed. Seam allowances are ¼″ unless otherwise noted.

1. Pair up the 6 print fabrics, choosing 2 fabrics for each of the 3 star blocks.

2. Using 2 squares from each of the 2 fabrics for a single block, make 4 half-square triangles (see Half-Square Triangles, page 73). Trim to 3½″ square.

Make 4.

Tip

I have found that by pressing seams open on half-square triangle units, the finished units are more accurate.

3. Using 4 matching background squares and the remaining medium/dark print fabric squares, make 8 half-square triangles, 4 of each fabric.

Make 4 of each.

4. Arrange the 12 half-square triangles and 4 matching 3½″ × 3½″ background squares as shown. Sew the units together in rows. Press.

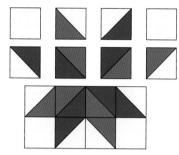

Block assembly

5. Repeat Steps 1–4 to make 3 blocks. Note in the quilt photo (page 29) that red is in the opposite position in one of the blocks.

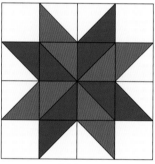

Make 3.

Runner Assembly

1. Arrange and sew the 3 blocks together with the 1½″ × 12½″ sashing strips, beginning and ending with a sashing strip. Press the seams toward the sashing.

2. Sew the 1½″ × 40½″ strips to the long edges of the runner. Press toward the strips.

3. Sew the 3½″ × 14½″ outer border strips to the short ends of the runner. Press the seams toward the outer borders.

4. Sew the 3½″ × 40″ outer border strips together to make a long strip. Cut 2 strips 46½″ long. Sew the strips to the long edges of the runner. Press the seams toward the outer borders.

5. Layer the backing, batting, and runner top. Quilt as desired. Bind the edges (see Binding, pages 76 and 77).

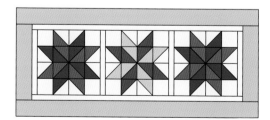

Runner assembly

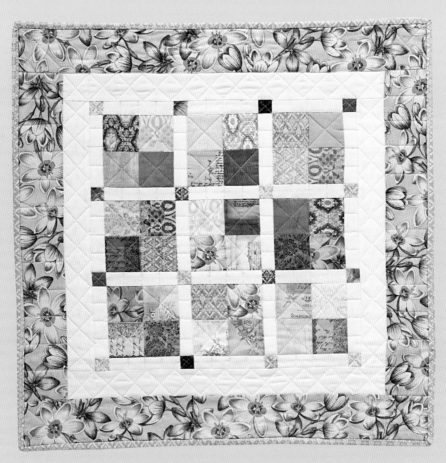

Pieced by Sherri McConnell and quilted by Gail Begay
Fabric collection: Curio by Basic Grey for Moda

Picture Windows Table Topper

Finished block: 4″ × 4″ • Finished table topper: 24″ × 24″

This table topper was constructed using a mini Charm Pack—a collection of 42 small 2½″ squares. As small as they are, the mini Charm Squares were cut to make the sashing squares. It's amazing what you can do with small squares or scraps!

Fabrics

Assorted prints and solids: ¼ yard total

Cream: ⅓ yard

Floral print: ⅜ yard

Backing: ⅞ yard

Binding: ⅓ yard

Batting: 30″ × 30″

Cutting

Assorted print and solid fabrics:
- Cut 36 squares 2½″ × 2½″ for Four-Patches.
- Cut 16 squares 1½″ × 1½″ for sashing squares.

Cream fabric:
- Cut 3 strips 1½″ × width of fabric; subcut into 24 strips 1½″ × 4½″ for sashing.
- Cut 2 strips 2″ × width of fabric; subcut into 2 strips 2″ × 16½″ and 2 strips 2″ × 19½″ for inner borders.

Floral print fabric:
- Cut 3 strips 3″ × width of fabric; subcut into 2 strips 3″ × 19½″ and 2 strips 3″ × 24½″ for outer borders.

Binding fabric:
- Cut 3 strips 2¼″ × width of fabric.

Block Assembly

Refer to The Basics (pages 70–77) as needed. Seam allowances are ¼″ unless otherwise noted.

Sew 4 squares 2½″ × 2½″ together to make a Four-Patch block. Make 9.

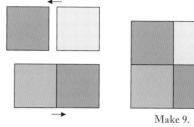

Make 9.

Table Topper Assembly

1. Arrange the Four-Patch blocks in 3 rows of 3 blocks each. Sew the blocks into rows, alternating them with 4 cream 1½″ × 4½″ sashing strips. Begin and end the row with a sashing strip. Press the seams toward the cream sashing. Make 3 rows.

2. Using 4 of the 1½″ × 1½″ squares and 3 of the 1½″ × 4½″ strips, make a sashing row, beginning and ending with a square. Press the seams toward the cream fabrics. Make 4.

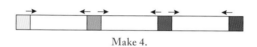

Make 4.

3. Sew the sashing rows and Four-Patch rows together; sew a sashing row to the top and bottom. Press the seams toward the sashing rows.

4. Sew the 2″ × 16½″ inner border strips to the left and right sides of the table topper. Press the seams toward the inner borders. Sew the 2″ × 19½″ inner border strips to the top and bottom of the table topper. Press the seams toward the inner borders.

5. Sew the 3″ × 19½″ border strips to the left and right sides of the table topper. Press the seams toward the borders. Sew the 3″ × 24½″ border strips to the top and bottom of the table topper. Press the seams toward the borders.

6. Layer the backing, batting, and top. Quilt as desired. Bind the edges (see Binding, pages 76 and 77).

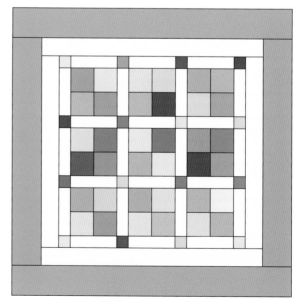

Table topper assembly

Carry-Alls

You can never have too many bags—and of course you need several different sizes according to what you take with you for the day.

In this section I share two of my go-to designs for bags—both roomy enough to take along everything you might need for an afternoon away, but neither so big that they are a bother to carry. They are perfect for showcasing your favorite fabric collections and can be made using a Charm Pack and a few additional fabrics.

Pieced and quilted by Sherri McConnell
Fabric collection: Sew Cherry by Lori Holt of Bee
in My Bonnet for Riley Blake

Hexagon Tote

Finished bag: 11¾″ high × 13½″ wide × 3″ deep

I really wanted to make a tote bag with hexagons and searched to find a pattern. When I couldn't find a pattern, I decided to design one myself! This is the first bag I designed. I love that you can make it from just one Charm Pack, and I love being able to use so many of my favorite fabrics in one bag.

Fabrics

Assorted prints: 1 Charm Pack— at least 39 squares 5″ × 5″

Top band fabric: ⅛ yard

Lining and handle fabric: ¾ yard (for lining, closure tab, pocket, and handle)

ByAnnie's Soft and Stable (or batting and interfacing):* 1 rectangle 18″ × 30″

Interfacing: 2 strips 2″ × 27″ medium-weight interfacing (fusible or nonfusible), such as Shape-Flex

* ByAnnie's Soft and Stable gives a structured shape to bags, making them very sturdy. You can use batting and interfacing instead, if desired. Shape-Flex or interfacing should be used for bag handles because ByAnnie's Soft and Stable makes the handle too bulky.

Notions

Templates: Marti Michell Perfect Patchwork Templates Set G or template plastic

Covered button kit: 1⅛″ (or 1⅛″-diameter button)

Cutting

Assorted prints:
- Cut 36 hexagons.**
- Cut 6 half-hexagons.***

Band fabric:
- Cut 1 strip 2½″ × width of fabric for the top bands; subcut into 2 strips 2½″ × 17½″.

Lining and handle fabric:
- Cut 2 strips 3″ × 27″ for handles.
- Cut 1 piece 17½″ × 26½″ for lining.
- Cut 1 piece 1½″ × 5″ for closure tab.
- Cut 2 pieces 5½″ × 8″ for pocket.

** Make a template from template plastic using the hexagon pattern (page 37) or use template 42 from Marti Michell's Template Set G. With a pencil, mark dots at the ¼″ seam intersections on the wrong side of fabric.

*** Make a template from template plastic using the half-hexagon pattern (page 37) or use template 43 from Marti Michell's Template Set G. Mark the ¼″ seam intersections on the wrong side of the fabric.

Bag Body Construction

Refer to The Basics (pages 70–77) as needed. Seam allowances are ¼″ unless otherwise noted.

1. Arrange the assorted hexagons and half-hexagons in 6 vertical rows as shown.

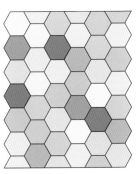

Arrange hexagons.

2. Sew the hexagons in each vertical row together, matching the dots. Begin and end the stitching at the marked dots, backstitching at each end. Do *not* stitch past the marks into the seam allowances. Press the seams in one direction. Make 6 vertical rows.

3. Sew the rows together, aligning the dots and sewing between them. Be careful not to sew into the seam allowances. Press the seams in the direction they naturally want to go.

4. Trim the bag body to 17½″ × 23″.

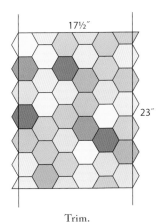

17½″

23″

Trim.

5. Sew the 2½″ × 17½″ top bands to the short ends of the bag body. Press the seams toward the bands.

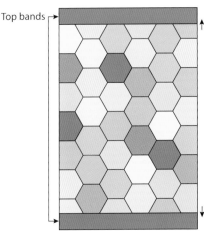

Top bands →

Add top bands.

6. Center the bag body over the ByAnnie's Soft and Stable (or batting and interfacing). Quilt as desired. I quilted a scant ¼″ away from each side of the 5 vertical seams. I also quilted the top bands ¼″ away from the seam between the band and hexagons. Trim to 17½″ × 27″.

Handle Construction

1. Center a 2″ × 27″ interfacing strip on the wrong side of a 3″ × 27″ handle strip. Press the long edges of the handle strips over the edges of the interfacing.

Center interfacing on handle.

2. Fold the strip in half lengthwise and press again. Stitch ⅛″ from both long edges to make the handle. Make 2.

Stitch handle.

Closure Tab Construction

1. Press the 1½″ × 5″ piece of fabric in half, wrong sides together.

2. Open up and press each long edge to the center fold line.

3. Fold in half again and topstitch ⅛″ from the long edges.

Bag Construction

1. Pin the raw edges of the handle to the short edges of the bag 3¾″ from each long edge of the bag body. Baste the handles in place ⅛″ from the edge.

2. Center the raw edges of the closure tab together at the top of the bag back and baste in place ⅛″ from the edge.

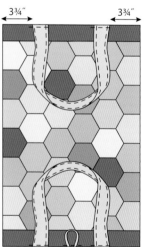

Baste handles and tab.

3. Fold the bag body in half, right sides together. Sew the sides using a ½″ seam allowance.

4. Place the 5½″ × 8″ pocket pieces right sides together and sew, using a ¼″ seam allowance. Leave a 3″ opening to turn the pocket right side out. Turn the pocket right side out and press well.

5. Center and pin the pocket to the right side of the lining, 3½″ down from the top of the lining. Sew around the 3 side edges, being sure to close the opening left from turning the pocket in Step 4. Also stitch 3½″ from one side of the pocket edge to make a divided pocket. Backstitch at the top edges of all pocket stitching.

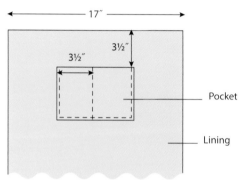

Stitch pocket.

6. Fold the lining fabric in half, right sides together, and sew the sides using a ½″ seam allowance, leaving a 4″ opening on one side to turn the bag right side out when finished.

7. To box the corners of the bag and lining, make a crease along the bottom of the bag and lining to mark the center. Fold the corner as shown so that it creates a point, and align the side seam with the crease. Measure in 1½″ and draw a line 3″ long. Pin and sew along the marked line. Sew again to reinforce the seam. Trim the corner, ¼″ from the stitching. Turn right side out and press well.

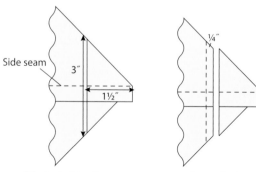

Mark stitching line.   Sew and trim.

8. Insert the bag body into the lining, right sides together. Match the side seams and sew the lining to the bag body along the top edge of the band using a ¼″ seam allowance. Be sure to catch the tops of the handles securely in the seam. You may want to stitch the handles twice to reinforce the seam.

9. Turn the bag right side out through the opening in the lining. Slipstitch the opening closed.

10. Press again, and stitch around the band ¼″ away from the top edge.

11. Cover the button, following the directions on the covered-button package (or use a purchased 1½″-diameter button). Sew the button to the bag front so that the bag closure loop fits around it.

Shortcut

To save time, you can purchase handles for your tote. Attach purchased handles by hand or machine after the bag is completed.

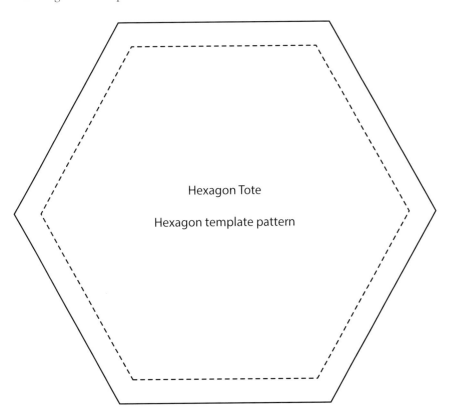

Hexagon Tote

Hexagon template pattern

Storing Patterns

Quilters seem to accumulate patterns along with fabric. I use a few different methods to store and organize my patterns. When I want to keep a pattern from a magazine, I cut out the pages and place them in sheet protectors. Then I file them in a binder according to pattern type. I have a binder for bags, one for pillows, one for large quilts, one for wall-hangings, and so on. I place patterns that I think I might want to make right away in a basket on my sewing table. I also have a collection of mini patterns that are about a quarter the size of regular patterns. I store these in little fabric baskets I made that are just the right size for the patterns.

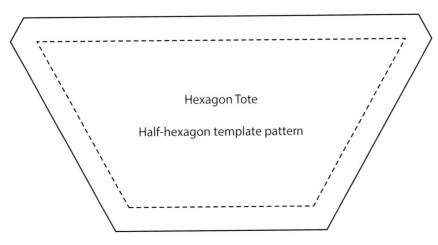

Hexagon Tote

Half-hexagon template pattern

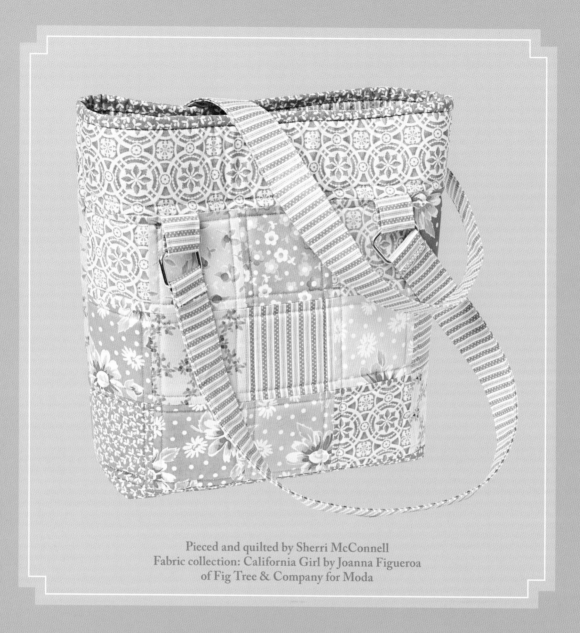

Pieced and quilted by Sherri McConnell
Fabric collection: California Girl by Joanna Figueroa
of Fig Tree & Company for Moda

Everyday Bag

Finished bag: 11½˝ high × 14˝ wide × 5˝ deep

This bag is also designed to showcase fabulous fabrics. I love the patchwork, and the binding and purchased handle rings give it a polished and professional look.

Fabrics

Coordinating prints: ½ yard total or 1 Charm Pack

Contrast fabric 1: ¼ yard

Contrast fabric 2: 1 yard

Binding: ⅛ yard

ByAnnie's Soft and Stable (or batting and interfacing):* 1 rectangle 17″ × 30″

Interfacing: 2 strips 2½″ × 26″ medium-weight (fusible or nonfusible) interfacing, such as Shape-Flex

ByAnnie's Soft and Stable gives a structured shape to bags, making them very sturdy. You can use batting and interfacing instead, if desired. Shape-Flex or interfacing should be used for bag handles because ByAnnie's Soft and Stable makes the handle too bulky.

Notions

Rings: 4 rectangular rings 1″ × 1½″

Cutting

Coordinating print fabrics:
- Cut 30 squares 3½″ × 3½″.

Contrast fabric 1:
- Cut 2 strips 3″ × 15½″ for top bands.

Contrast fabric 2:
- Cut 1 rectangle 15½″ × 28″ for lining.
- Cut 1 rectangle 7″ × 12″ for pocket.
- Cut 2 strips 3½″ × 27″ for handles.
- Cut 1 strip 4½″ × 12½″ for handle tabs.
- Cut 1 rectangle 5½″ × 15½″ for bag bottom.

Binding fabric:
- Cut 1 strip 2¼″ × width of fabric.

Bag Assembly

Refer to The Basics (pages 70–77) as needed. Seam allowances are ¼″ unless otherwise noted.

1. Sew the 3½″ × 3½″ squares together into 3 rows of 5 squares each. Make 2 rectangles of 3 rows each.

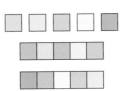

Make 2.

2. Make handle tabs by folding the 4½″ × 12½″ rectangle in half, wrong sides together. Open the rectangle and press each long outer edge to the middle. Fold in half, enclosing the raw edges. Stitch along both edges. Cut into 4 segments, each 3″ long.

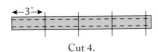

Cut 4.

3. Wrap each of the 4 handle tabs around one of the rectangular bag rings. Pin both raw edges of the handle tab to the top of the bag rectangles from Step 1, placing the tabs 3½″ in from the side edges. Baste in place ⅛″ from the edge.

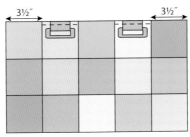

Baste handle tabs.

4. Sew a 3″ × 15½″ top band to the top of each bag unit, right sides together, being sure

to catch the handle tabs securely in the seam allowance. Press the seam toward the top band.

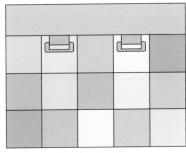

Sew band to bag.

5. Sew the 5½″ × 15½″ bag bottom between the units from Step 4 to join the front and back of the bag. Press the seams toward the bag bottom.

Sew bag bottom to front and back.

6. Center the bag body over the ByAnnie's Soft and Stable (or batting and interfacing). Quilt as desired. I quilted ¼″ straight lines on both sides of each seam. I also quilted ¼″ from the top and bottom band seams. Trim to 15½″ × 28½″.

7. Make the bag handles by centering the 2½″ × 25″ strips of interfacing on the 3½″ × 26″ strips of handle fabric. Fold the short ends over the interfacing and press. Press the long edges of the handle fabric over the interfacing (and over the turned-under ends).

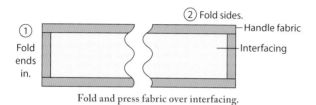

Fold and press fabric over interfacing.

8. Fold the handle in half, press, and stitch along both long edges. Make 2.

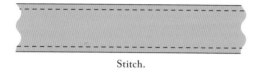

Stitch.

9. Wrap one end of the handle around a rectangular ring and pin in place. Wrap the other end of the handle around the other rectangular ring on the bag unit. Stitch the handles in place, sewing through both layers of the handle. Repeat with the other side of the bag unit. Make sure the handles on both sides are the same length.

10. Sew the sides of the bag, right sides together, using a ½″ seam allowance. To box the corners, make a crease to mark the center of the bag bottom. Fold the corner so that it creates a point and align the side seam with the crease. Measure in 2½″ and draw a line 5″ long as shown. Pin and sew along the marked line. Sew again to reinforce the seam.

Trim the corner ¼″ from the stitching. Turn the bag right side out and press well.

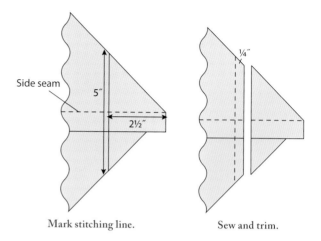

Mark stitching line.   Sew and trim.

11. Make the pocket by folding the 7″ × 12″ pocket rectangle in half, right sides together so that the pocket is 7″ × 6″. Sew along the 3 open sides, leaving an opening for turning. Turn the pocket inside out and press. Center the pocket on the lining, 3½″ down from the top edge. Sew the pocket to the lining as shown, backstitching at the beginning and end.

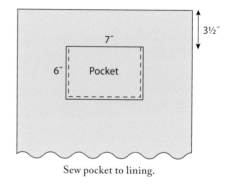

Sew pocket to lining.

12. Repeat Step 10 to sew the sides of the lining together and box the corners, but don't turn the lining right side out.

13. Insert the lining into the bag, wrong sides together. Pin the top edges. Bind the edges (see Binding, pages 76 and 77).

14. If desired, tack the bottom of the lining to the bag to secure it in place.

On the Wall

I still remember when my grandmother started hanging quilts on the walls of her home. In fact, I remember when she told me that these "wall quilts" were called "wallhangings." Pretty soon, most of the households in our family were doing some decorating with wall quilts, mostly because my grandmother made and presented beautiful wallhangings as gifts. Quilts of nearly any size can function as a wallhanging. If I know I'm going to use a quilt primarily as a wallhanging I don't wash it, preferring it to have a more crisp appearance. The wall quilts in this chapter are a little on the large size, and they work well as a focal point in a room or on a wall. But really, any small quilt can work as a wallhanging!

Pieced by Sherri McConnell and quilted by Andrea Marquez
Fabric collections: Vintage Modern by Bonnie & Camille for Moda; Bella Solids by Moda

Grandma's Garden

Finished block: 10″ × 12″ • *Finished quilt:* 43″ × 49″

My grandmother loves flowers and has always cultivated a beautiful flower garden.
Now in her 90s, she isn't really able to garden anymore, so this flower garden is for her.

Fabrics

Assorted red, pink, and aqua prints: ½ yard total

Assorted green prints: ⅜ yard total

Assorted gray prints: ⅔ yard total

White: 1¾ yards

Backing: 3 yards

Binding:* ½ yard

Batting: 49″ × 55″

* The binding on the quilt shown is a scrappy binding made with extra Jelly Roll strips. See Scrappy Binding (page 76).

Jelly Roll option:

This quilt can easily be made using a Jelly Roll (a precut roll of 40 strips, 2½″ × width of fabric, offered by many fabric companies). You might need to add some ⅛- or ¼-yard pieces to have enough greens, reds, and grays, depending on the Jelly Roll you purchase and the colors you want to use. To make the quilt as shown in the photo (previous page), you will need the following:

3 red prints: 1 Jelly Roll strip of each

2 pink prints: 1 Jelly Roll strip of each

2 aqua prints: 1 Jelly Roll strip of each

3 green prints: 2 Jelly Roll strips of each

5 gray prints: 2 Jelly Roll strips of each

Cutting

Assorted red, pink, and aqua print fabrics:
- Cut 9 matching sets of 1 square 2½″ × 2½″ and 2 rectangles 2½″ × 4½″ for tulip blocks.
- Cut 16 red squares 2½″ × 2½″ for post squares.

Assorted green print fabrics:
- Cut 9 matching sets of 2 squares 2½″ × 2½″ and 2 rectangles 2½″ × 4½″ for leaves and stems.

Assorted gray print fabrics:
- Cut 12 strips 2½″ × 12½″ and 12 strips 2½″ × 10½″ for sashing.

White fabric:
- Cut 17 strips 2½″ × width of fabric for block backgrounds; subcut into:

  18 rectangles 2½″ × 10½″

  36 rectangles 2½″ × 4½″

  81 squares 2½″ × 2½″

- Cut 5 strips 3″ × width of fabric for border.

Binding fabric:
- Cut 5 strips 2¼″ × width of fabric.

Block Assembly

Refer to The Basics (pages 70–77) as needed. Seam allowances are ¼″ unless otherwise noted.

1. Sew a white 2½″ × 2½″ square to a red 2½″ × 2½″ square.

2. Make the Flying Geese units using 1 red 2½″ × 4½″ rectangle with 2 white 2½″ × 2½″ squares. Draw a diagonal line from corner to corner on the wrong side of each white square. Align a square on one end of the rectangle and stitch on the line. Trim the seam allowance to ¼″ and press (see Corner-Square Triangles, page 74). Repeat on the opposite side of the rectangle to complete the Flying Geese unit. Make 2.

3. Sew a Flying Geese unit from Step 2 to each side of the unit from Step 1.

4. Sew a 2½″ × 4½″ white rectangle to each side of the unit from Step 3.

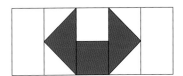

Organizing Projects

I've tried many different ways to organize my quilt-making projects. While some projects may be completed in a short time, every quilter seems to have those projects they like to work on occasionally or have ready to work on at a moment's notice. Scrapbook storage boxes that are 12″ × 12″ are great for storing works in progress. Plastic shoeboxes also work well. I often keep take-along projects in plastic zipper bags so I can grab them at a moment's notice. At one time I even had a lot of my projects stored in pizza boxes purchased from a pizza shop! Pizza boxes stack well on shelves, don't take up too much room, and are easy to label.

Whatever method you decide to use to organize ongoing projects, I suggest that you keep a list of everything you have stored along with where it is stored. This way your ongoing projects won't turn into the dreaded UFOs—unfinished objects—that get lost, only to reappear years later after you've lost interest in them.

Photo by Korindi Olson Totten

5. Place a white 2½″ × 2½″ square on one side of a green 2½″ × 4½″ rectangle, right sides together. Draw a diagonal line from corner to corner on the wrong side of the white square and stitch on the line. Trim the seam allowance to ¼″ and press (see Corner-Square Triangles, page 74). Repeat on the opposite side of the rectangle as shown, using another 2½″ × 2½″ white square.

6. Repeat Step 5 to make a mirror image of the leaf unit.

7. Sew together a unit from Step 5, a green 2½″ × 2½″ square, and a unit from Step 6.

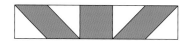

8. Sew 2 white 2½″ × 4½″ rectangles to opposite sides of a green 2½″ × 2½″ square.

9. Sew the units from Steps 4, 7, and 8 together with 2 white 2½″ × 10½″ rectangles as shown.

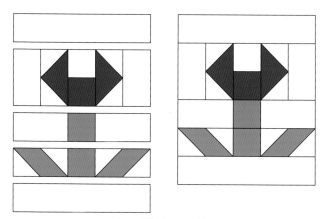

Tulip block assembly

10. Repeat Steps 1–9 to make 9 tulip blocks.

Quilt Assembly

1. Arrange the blocks in 3 rows of 3 blocks each, alternating them with the gray 2½″ × 12½″ sashing strips. Begin and end each row with a sashing strip. Sew the blocks and sashing together. Press the seams toward the sashing.

2. Sew 4 sashing rows using 4 red 2½″ × 2½″ squares and 3 gray 2½″ × 10½″ sashing strips. Begin and end each sashing row with a red square. Press the seams toward the gray sashing strips.

3. Sew the sashing rows and the tulip block rows together. Press the seams toward the sashing rows.

4. Sew the 5 white 3″ × 42″ border strips together to make 1 strip. Cut into 2 strips 3″ × 44½″ for the side borders and 2 strips 3″ × 43½″ for the top and bottom.

5. Add the border strips to the sides and then the top and bottom of the quilt. Press the seams toward the borders.

6. Layer the backing, batting, and quilt top. Quilt as desired. Bind the edges (see Binding, pages 76 and 77).

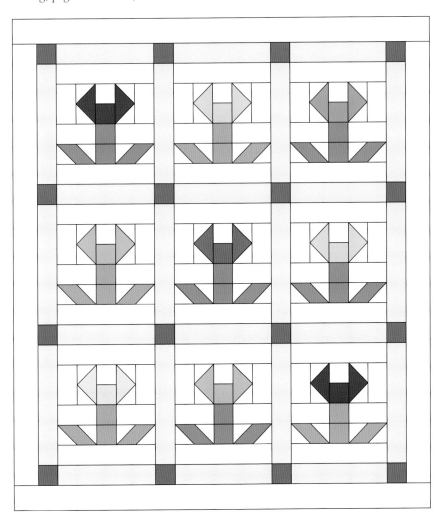

Quilt assembly

45

Grandma's Garden

Pieced by Sherri McConnell and quilted by Andrea Marquez
Fabric collection: Good Fortune by Kate Spain for Moda

Water Lily

***Finished block:** 8½″ × 8½″* • ***Finished quilt:** 54½″ × 54½″*

I fell in love with these fabrics at first sight. I kept thinking of Monet's beautiful water lily paintings and wanted to create the same type of effect by my arrangement of color in this quilt. Although these fabrics present a very peaceful, tranquil effect, this quilt would be equally stunning in bright, bold fabrics and geometric prints.

Fabrics

Assorted prints: 25
Layer Cake squares
(10″ × 10″ squares)

White: 1⅝ yards

Border: ⅞ yard

Backing: 3½ yards

Binding: ½ yard

Batting: 61″ × 61″

Cutting

Layer Cake print squares:
- Cut 4 squares 4″ × 4″ and
  1 square 2″ × 2″ from each.

White fabric:
- Cut 20 strips 2″ × width
  of fabric; subcut into
  100 rectangles 2″ × 4″
  and 200 squares 2″ × 2″.
- Cut 5 strips 2½″ × width
  of fabric.

Border fabric:
- Cut 6 strips 4½″ × width
  of fabric.

Binding fabric:
- Cut 6 strips 2¼″ × width
  of fabric.

Block Assembly

Refer to The Basics (pages 70–77) as needed. Seam allowances are ¼″ unless otherwise noted.

1. Draw a diagonal line from corner to corner on the wrong side of the white 2″ × 2″ squares. Place a white 2″ × 2″ square on the corner of a print 4″ × 4″ square, right sides together. Use the Corner-Square Triangles technique (page 74) to add white triangles to 2 opposite corners of all of the print 4″ squares as shown. Make 100.

Make 100.

2. Sew together 4 matching units from Step 1, a matching 2″ square, and 4 white 2″ × 4″ rectangles as shown. Make 25.

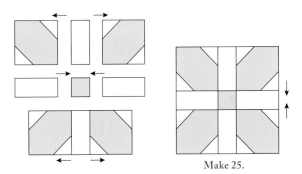

Make 25.

Quilt Assembly

1. Arrange the blocks in 5 rows of 5 blocks each. Sew the blocks in each row together. Press the seams in opposite direction from row to row. Sew the rows together and press.

2. Piece the 5 white 2½″ × 42″ inner border strips together and cut into 2 strips 2½″ × 43″ for the sides and 2 strips 2½″ × 47″ for the top and bottom of the quilt. Sew the borders to the quilt and press the seams toward the borders.

3. Piece the 6 strips 4½″ × 42″ for the outer border together and cut into 2 strips 4½″ × 47″ for the sides and 2 strips 4½″ × 55″ for the top and bottom of the quilt. Sew the borders to the quilt and press the seams toward the borders.

4. Layer the backing, batting, and quilt top. Quilt as desired. Bind the edges (see Binding, pages 76 and 77).

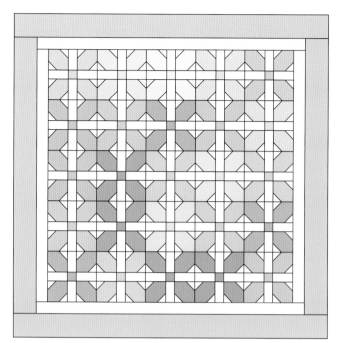

Quilt layout

Pieced by Sherri McConnell and quilted by Gail Begay
Fabric collection: Verona by Emily Taylor Design for Riley Blake

Quilts around the House

Nothing says home quite like having quilts around to create beauty and add that special sense of warmth to any decor. Whether traditional or modern in design, quilts always seem to say, "This is home." The quilts in this section can serve a variety of purposes. *Pinwheel Picnic* is just the right size to use as a wallhanging or table topper. *Parlor*, *Vintage Snowballs*, and *Newport* are just right for displaying on the couch to use as throw quilts.

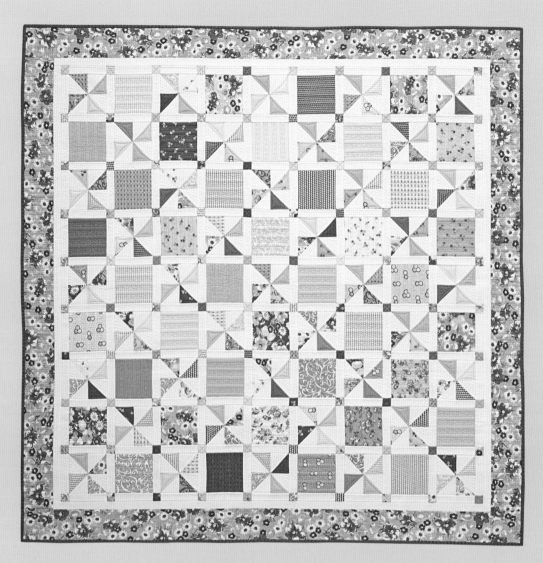

Pieced by Sherri McConnell and quilted by Judi Madsen
Fabric collection: Ruby by Bonnie & Camille for Moda

Pinwheel Picnic

Finished block: 4½″ × 4½″ • **Finished quilt:** 58½″ × 58½″

This is the first larger quilt I designed. I really wanted to make a scrappy Pinwheel block to combine with Charm Squares, so I designed the pinwheels to finish at 4½″ square so that the Charm Squares wouldn't have to be trimmed at all for the alternate blocks. I love the mix of fabrics in this design.

Fabrics

Assorted prints: 4 Charm Square packs, or 1 Layer Cake (40 squares 10˝ × 10˝), or 1¾ yards total

White: 2⅜ yards

Border: ¾ yard

Backing: 3¾ yards

Binding: ½ yard

Batting: 65˝ × 65˝

Cutting

See the cutting diagram below if using Layer Cake squares. Note that you will need to cut 1 extra 3½˝ square from 2 of the Layer Cake squares for a total of 82 squares.

Assorted print fabrics:
- Cut 40 squares 5˝ × 5˝ for alternate blocks.
- Cut 82 squares 3½˝ × 3½˝ for Pinwheel blocks.
- Cut 100 squares 1½˝ × 1½˝ for corner posts.

White fabric:
- Cut 8 strips 3½˝ × width of fabric; subcut into 82 squares 3½˝ × 3½˝ for Pinwheel blocks.
- Cut 23 strips 1½˝ × width of fabric; subcut into 180 rectangles 1½˝ × 5˝ for sashing.
- Cut 6 strips 1½˝ × width of fabric for inner borders.

Border fabric:
- Cut 6 strips 3½˝ × width of fabric for outer borders.

Binding fabric:
- Cut 7 strips 2¼˝ × width of fabric.

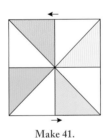

Cutting guide for Layer Cake squares

Block Assembly

Refer to The Basics (pages 70–77) as needed. Seam allowances are ¼˝ unless otherwise noted.

1. Place 1 white and 1 print 3½˝ × 3½˝ square right sides together. Make half-square triangle units (page 73). Trim the half-square triangles units to 2¾˝ × 2¾˝. Make 164.

Make 164.

Trimming Made Easy

Monique Dillard's Fit to Be Quarter ruler is the ideal tool for trimming these half-square triangle units. See Resources (page 78).

2. Sew together 4 half-square triangle units to make a Pinwheel block. Make 41.

Make 41.

Displaying Quilts

Displaying quilts in your home is one of the best parts about being a quilter! Quilts seem to add something that no other decorations can—that homemade element of personalization. Some of my favorite ways to display quilts are to drape them over chairs and sofas, use them as table toppers, set them diagonally on a trunk or table, stack them on a shelf, place them in a display cabinet, roll them up and place them in baskets and in large crocks or bins, and, of course, hang them on the wall!

Quilt Assembly

1. Beginning with a Pinwheel block, arrange the blocks and the 5″ × 5″ squares in 9 rows of 9 blocks each, leaving space for sashing between them. When you are pleased with the arrangement, add 1½″ × 5″ white sashing strips to the rows. Block rows should begin and end with a white sashing strip.

2. Sew the Pinwheel blocks, sashing strips, and squares into rows.

3. Sew a sashing row using 10 of the 1½″ × 1½″ print squares and 9 of the 1½″ × 5″ white sashing strips. Begin and end the sashing row with a 1½″ × 1½″ square. Make 10 rows.

Make 10.

4. Sew a sashing row between each block row. Sew a sashing row to the top and bottom of the quilt.

5. Piece the 1½″ × 42″ inner border strips together and cut 2 strips 1½″ × 51″ for the sides and 2 strips 1½″ × 53″ for the top and bottom of the quilt.

6. Sew the inner border strips to the sides and then the top and bottom of the quilt. Press the seams toward the inner borders.

7. Piece the 3½″ × 42″ border strips together and cut 2 strips 3½″ × 53″ for the sides and 2 strips 3½″ × 59″ for the top and bottom of the quilt.

8. Sew the outer border strips to the sides and then the top and bottom of the quilt. Press the seams toward the outer borders.

9. Layer the backing, batting, and quilt top. Quilt as desired. Bind the edges (see Binding, pages 76 and 77).

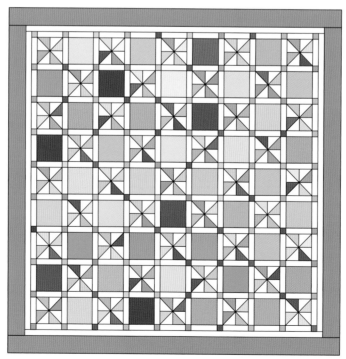
Quilt assembly

Pieced by Sherri McConnell and quilted by Andrea Marquez
Fabric collection: Curio by Basic Grey for Moda

Parlor

Finished block: 10″ × 10″ • *Finished quilt:* 70″ × 70″

This quilt was really inspired by the fabric. I first saw this collection
at International Quilt Market in Salt Lake City during the spring
of 2011. While the vintage charm of the muted colors reminded
me of my great-grandmother's home in Cedar Rapids, Iowa,
there is also something very modern about this collection.

Fabrics

Assorted prints and solids: 1 fat-eighth bundle or scraps to total 3½ yards

Cream: 1⅓ yards

Border: 1⅛ yards

Backing: 4¼ yards

Binding: ⅝ yard

Batting: 76″ × 76″

Cutting

Assorted print/solid fabrics:
- Cut 36 squares 4½″ × 4½″ for block centers.
- Cut 36 matching sets of 2 rectangles 2½″ × 6½″ and 2 rectangles 2½″ × 10½″ for blocks.

Cream fabric:
- Cut 21 strips 1½″ × width of fabric; subcut into 72 rectangles 1½″ × 4½″ and 72 rectangles 1½″ × 6½″ for blocks.
- Cut 7 strips 1½″ × width of fabric for inner border.

Border fabric:
- Cut 7 strips 4½″ × width of fabric.

Binding fabric:
- Cut 8 strips 2¼″ × width of fabric.

Block Assembly

Refer to The Basics (pages 70–77) as needed. Seam allowances are ¼″ unless otherwise noted.

1. Sew a 1½″ × 4½″ cream rectangle to opposite sides of a 4½″ × 4½″ print square. Press the seams toward the cream fabric. Sew a 1½″ × 6½″ cream rectangle to the top and bottom. Press.

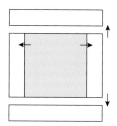

2. Sew 2½″ × 6½″ print/solid strips to the sides of the block unit. Press the seams toward the outer strips. Sew the matching 2½″ × 10½″ print or solid strips to the top and bottom. Press. Make a total of 36 blocks.

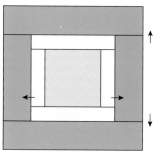

Make 36.

A Perfect Fit

One way to make sure you have quilts for all of those special places just calling out for something soft and colorful is to walk around your home and make a list of the places you really want to decorate with quilts. On my list, I've included possible size ranges for projects that would fit with specific spots in my home. With this list, I can alter patterns if necessary to make something that will fit a specific spot rather than completing a project and then wishing I'd made it just a little bigger or smaller.

Quilt Assembly

1. Arrange the blocks into 6 rows of 6 blocks each. Turn every other block so that the block seams do not have to be matched. Stitch the blocks in each row together. Press the seams in opposite direction from row to row. Sew the rows together and press.

2. Piece the 1½″ × 42″ inner border strips together and cut into 2 lengths 1½″ × 60½″ for the sides of the quilt and 2 strips 1½″ × 62½″ for the top and bottom.

3. Sew the inner borders to the sides and then the top and bottom of the quilt. Press the seams toward the border fabric.

4. Sew the 4½″ × 42″ outer border strips together and cut into 2 lengths 4½″ × 62½″ for the sides of the quilt and 2 lengths 4½″ × 70½″ for the top and bottom.

5. Sew the outer borders to the sides and then the top and bottom of the quilt. Press the seams toward the outer borders.

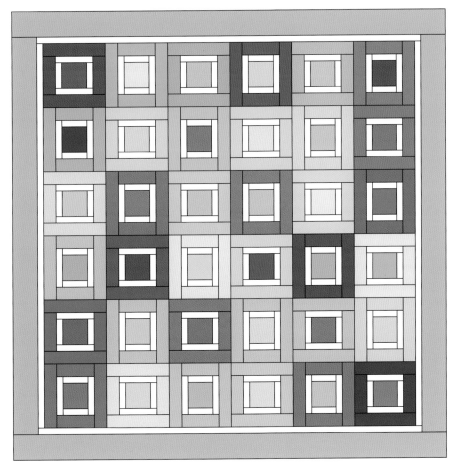

Quilt assembly

6. Layer the backing, batting, and quilt top. Quilt as desired. Bind the edges (see Binding, pages 76 and 77).

Pieced by Sherri McConnell and quilted by Andrea Marquez
Fabric collection: Circa 1934 by Cosmo Cricket for Moda

Vintage Snowballs

Finished block: *10″ × 10″* • ***Finished quilt:*** *73″ × 83″*

I've always loved the Snowball block, but I don't love worrying about matching seams when putting them together. I designed this quilt with the sashing on two sides to be able to put Snowball blocks together with no seams to worry about! The whimsical feel of the design seemed perfect for another "vintage modern" fabric collection!

Fabrics

Assorted prints:
1 Layer Cake (or
42 squares 10″ × 10″)

Cream: 3½ yards

Red: ⅜ yard

Border print: 1⅓ yards

Backing: 5⅛ yards

Binding: ⅔ yard

Batting: 80″ × 90″

Cutting

Assorted print fabrics:
- Cut 42 squares
  8½″ × 8½″ for blocks.

Cream fabric:
- Cut 13 strips 3″ × width
  of fabric; subcut
  into 168 squares
  3″ × 3″ for blocks.
- Cut 25 strips 2½″ × width
  of fabric; subcut into
  42 strips 2½″ × 8½″ and
  42 strips 2½″ × 10½″
  for sashing.
- Cut 7 strips 2½″ × width
  of fabric for inner borders.

Red fabric:
- Cut 7 strips 1½″ × width
  of fabric for narrow
  "peek" borders.

Border fabric:
- Cut 8 strips 5″ × width of
  fabric for outer borders.

Binding fabric:
- Cut 9 strips 2¼″ × width
  of fabric.

Block Assembly

Refer to The Basics (pages 70–77) as needed. Seam allowances are ¼″ unless otherwise noted.

1. Draw a diagonal line from corner to corner on the wrong side of the 3″ × 3″ cream squares. Refer to Corner-Square Triangles (page 74) to sew a marked square to each corner of the 8½″ × 8½″ print square. Make 42.

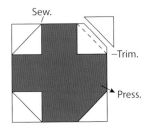

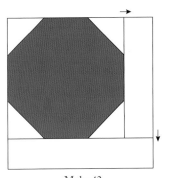

Make 42.

2. Sew a 2½″ × 8½″ rectangle to the right side of each Snowball unit. Press toward the rectangle. Sew a 2½″ × 10½″ rectangle to the bottom of each unit. Press. Make 42.

Make 42.

Making Do

My Layer Cake had a couple of light-colored squares that didn't provide enough contrast with the sashing fabric. I cut a few **Charm Squares** from the same fabric collection into 2½″ × 2½″ squares and sewed 16 of these together to make a scrappy, pieced block. I made two of these blocks and then added the cream squares to the corners. This turned out to be a great addition to the quilt. It's always fun to have a couple of blocks that are a little different; they add visual interest to your quilt.

Pieced Snowball block

Quilt Assembly

1. Arrange the blocks in 7 rows of 6 blocks each. After you have arranged the blocks in a pleasing manner, turn every other block 90°. By doing this you won't have any seams to match up when you sew the blocks together into rows. The snowballs will be staggered throughout the quilt, creating a more interesting and random look.

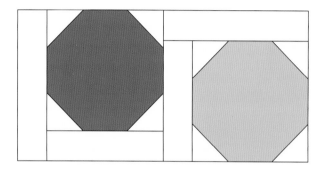

2. Sew the blocks together into rows. Press the seams in opposite direction from row to row. Sew the rows together and press.

3. Sew the cream 2½″ × 42″ inner border strips together and cut into 2 strips 2½″ × 70½″ for the sides of the quilt and 2 strips 2½″ × 64½″ for the top and bottom.

4. Sew the inner borders to the sides of the quilt and then to the top and bottom. Press the seams toward the inner borders.

5. Sew the red 1½″ × 42″ border strips together and cut into 2 strips 1½″ × 74½″ for the sides and 2 strips 1½″ × 64½″ for the top and bottom. Press the strips in half, wrong sides together, to make the peek borders (the strips will now measure ¾″ wide). Aligning the raw edges, sew the longer strips to the sides of the quilt with a ⅛″ seam. Align raw edges and sew the shorter strips to the top and bottom of the quilt, also with a ⅛″ seam. When the outer borders are added to the quilt, the seam will enclose the seam of the peek border.

6. Sew the print 5″ × 42″ outer border strips together and cut into 2 strips 5″ × 74½″ for the sides and 2 strips 5″ × 73½″ for the top and bottom. Sew the borders to the sides and then the top and bottom of the quilt. Press the seams toward the outer borders.

7. Layer the backing, batting, and quilt top. Quilt as desired. Bind the edges (see Binding, pages 76 and 77).

Quilt assembly

Adding a "Peek" Border

You can easily add a peek border to any quilt for extra pizzazz. It is sometimes called unfilled or flat piping. This border does not change the finished size of the quilt, because it lies flat on top of an existing border. Often, a peek border can add just the needed splash of color near the edge of a quilt. To figure out how much fabric you'll need for a peek border, add the lengths of the left, right, top, and bottom borders that the peek border will sit on top of. Divide this number by 40, and this will give you the number of strips you'll need. Multiply the number of strips by the width of strips you want to cut, usually 1½″. The result is how many inches of fabric you'll need.

Remember that peek borders are folded in half, wrong sides together, so double the width you want for your finished border and add ½″ for seam allowances. For a ½″ finished peek border, multiply by 2 and add ½″; you'll need to cut your strips 1½″ wide.

Pieced by Sherri McConnell and quilted by Andrea Marquez
Fabric collection: Secret Garden by Sandi Henderson for Michael Miller

Newport

Finished block: 7½″ × 7½″ • *Finished quilt:* 61½″ × 69″

This is a perfect design for allowing the fabrics to make the quilt. I couldn't bear to cut these beautiful floral prints into small pieces and really wanted to showcase each pattern from the collection. Since the flowers and the colors remind me of my favorite place to vacation, Newport Beach, California, it was natural to name this gorgeous quilt after a gorgeous place!

Fabrics

Assorted prints:* 3 yards total

Cream: 1⅝ yards

Border: ⅞ yard

Backing: 4 yards

Binding: ⅝ yard

Batting: 68″ × 75″

Two Layer Cakes (80 squares, 10″ × 10″) may be used for the block centers.

Cutting

Assorted print fabrics:
- Cut 56 squares 8″ × 8″ for blocks.

Cream fabric:
- Cut 11 strips 3½″ × width of fabric; subcut into 112 squares 3½″ × 3½″ for block corners.
- Cut 6 strips 2″ × width of fabric for inner borders.

Border fabric:
- Cut 7 strips 3½″ × width of fabric for outer borders.

Binding fabric:
- Cut 7 strips 2¼″ × width of fabric.

Block Assembly

Refer to The Basics (pages 70–77) as needed. Seam allowances are ¼″ unless otherwise noted.

Using the Corner-Square Triangles method (page 74), add a cream 3½″ × 3½″ square to opposite corners of each of the 8″ × 8″ print squares. Make 56.

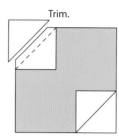
Trim.

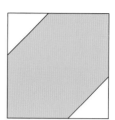
Make 56.

Quilt Assembly

1. Arrange the blocks in 8 rows of 7 blocks each. Sew the blocks together to make 8 rows. Press seams in opposite direction from row to row. Sew the rows together. Press.

2. Sew the 2″ × 42″ inner border strips together and cut into 2 strips 2″ × 60½″ for the sides and 2 strips 2″ × 56″ for the top and bottom.

3. Sew the side inner border strips and then the top and bottom border strips to the quilt. Press the seams toward the inner border.

4. Sew the 3½″ × 42″ outer border strips together and cut into 2 strips 3½″ × 63½″ for the sides and 2 strips 3½″ × 62″ for the top and bottom borders. Sew the side borders and then the top and bottom borders to the quilt. Press the seams toward the outer border.

5. Layer the backing, batting, and quilt top. Quilt as desired. Bind the edges (see Binding, pages 76 and 77).

Quilt assembly

In the Nursery

It seems I've been making baby quilts for gifts since I began making quilts. So many times when a quilt is given for a baby, the recipient is afraid to really use it! My grandmother always made a baby quilt to use as a wallhanging and another separate quilt to *really* use. The two quilts in this chapter are simple in design and can be used as beautiful wallhangings or as the baby quilt that gets used!

Pieced by Sherri McConnell and quilted by Andrea Marquez
Fabric collections: City Weekend and Cape Ann by Oliver & S. for Moda

Weathervane

Finished block: 12″ × 12″ • Finished quilt: 45″ × 45″

The Weathervane block and the Nine-Patch are two of my
favorite designs. Combining them in one fast, fun quilt opens
the door to endless fabric combinations. Mine is a scrappy
blue version, combining two different lines of fabric.

Fabrics

Assorted blue prints: 10 fat quarters

White: 1½ yards

Polka dot: ⅝ yard

Backing: 3 yards

Binding: ½ yard

Batting: 51″ × 51″

Cutting

5 blue print fabrics:
- Cut 1 square 4½″ × 4½″ *from each* for Weathervane blocks.
- Cut 4 squares 2⅞″ × 2⅞″ *from each* for Weathervane blocks.
- Cut 4 squares 2½″ × 2½″ *from each* for Weathervane blocks.

5 blue print fabrics:
- Cut 4 squares 4½″ × 4½″ *from each* for Weathervane blocks.

Remainder of blue print fabrics (or scraps):
- Cut 16 squares 4½″ × 4½″ for Nine-Patch blocks.

White fabric:
- Cut 2 strips 2⅞″ × width of fabric; subcut into 20 squares 2⅞″ × 2⅞″ for Weathervane blocks.
- Cut 4 strips 2½″ × width of fabric; subcut into 60 squares 2½″ × 2½″ for Weathervane blocks.
- Cut 3 strips 4½″ × width of fabric; subcut into 20 squares 4½″ × 4½″ for Nine-Patch blocks.
- Cut 2 strips 2″ × 36½″ for inner border.
- Cut 2 strips 2″ × 39½″ for inner border.

Polka-dot fabric:
- Cut 2 strips 3½″ × 39½″ for outer border.
- Cut 3 strips 3½″ × width of fabric for outer border.

Binding fabric:
- Cut 5 strips 2¼″ × width of fabric.

Weathervane Block Assembly

Refer to The Basics (pages 70–77) as needed. Seam allowances are ¼″ unless otherwise noted.

1. Using the Corner-Square Triangles technique (page 74), draw a diagonal line from corner to corner on the wrong side of 8 of the 2½″ × 2½″ white squares. Add a marked white square to each of 2 adjacent corners of a 4½″ × 4½″ blue print square. Press. Make 4 matching units.

Make 4.

2. Choose a second blue print and make half-square triangles (page 73) using 4 white 2⅞″ × 2⅞″ squares and 4 matching blue print 2⅞″ × 2⅞″ squares. Press. Make 8 half-square triangle units.

3. Make the block corner units using 2 half-square triangle units from Step 2, a white 2½″ × 2½″ square, and a matching blue print 2½″ × 2½″ square. Press. Make 4.

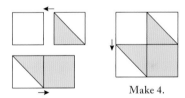

Make 4.

4. Sew together 4 units from Step 3, a blue print 4½″ square that matches the units from Steps 2 and 3, and 4 units from Step 1 to make the Weathervane block. Press. Repeat Steps 1–4 to make 5 blocks.

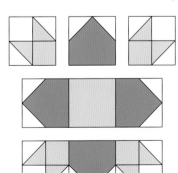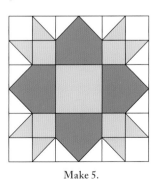

Make 5.

Nine-Patch Block Assembly

Sew 4 blue print 4½″ × 4½″ squares and 5 white 4½″ × 4½″ squares into a Nine-Patch block as shown. Press. Make 4.

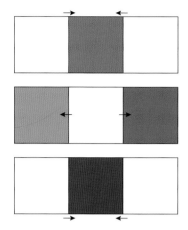

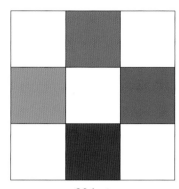

Make 4.

Quilt Assembly

1. Arrange and sew the blocks into 3 rows of 3 blocks each. Press the seams toward the Nine-Patch blocks. Sew the rows together. Press.

2. Sew the 2″ × 36½″ inner border strips to the sides of the quilt top. Press the seams toward the inner borders. Sew the 2″ × 39½″ inner border strips to the top and bottom and press.

3. Sew the 3½″ × 39½″ outer border strips to the sides of the quilt. Press the seams toward the outer borders.

4. Sew the 3½″ × 42″ outer border strips together and cut 2 strips 3½″ × 45½″ for the top and bottom of the quilt. Sew the strips to the quilt and press the seams toward the outer borders.

5. Layer the backing, batting, and quilt top. Quilt as desired. Bind the edges (see Binding, pages 76 and 77).

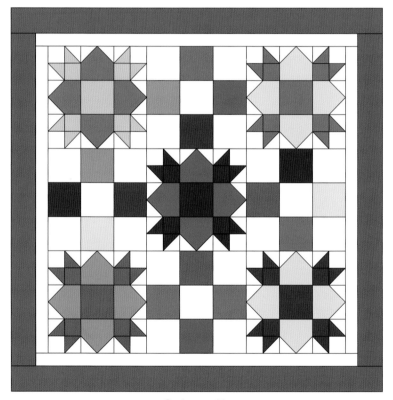

Quilt assembly

Pieced by Sherri McConnell and quilted by Andrea Marquez
Fabric collection: Fresh Palette by Carrie Nelson of Miss Rosie's Quilt Company for Henry Glass & Co.

Posies

Finished block: 12″ × 12″ • *Finished quilt:* 44½″ × 44½″

I had to have an Irish chain variation quilt in this book. After all, the Irish chain was the pattern I used for at least my first dozen quilts! This quilt is made feminine through the fabrics—perfect for a baby girl's nursery. It's simple to swap the prints and colors for a boy's quilt.

Fabrics

Assorted prints and solids:*
18 different fat eighths

White: 1⅜ yards

Border: ⅝ yard

Backing: 3 yards

Binding: ½ yard

Batting: 51″ × 51″

You can also use 9 fat eighths and 9 Charm Squares (5″ × 5″ squares).

Cutting

9 assorted print fabrics:
· Cut 1 square 4½″ × 4½″ *from each* for block centers.

9 assorted print fabrics:
· Cut 8 squares 2½″ × 2½″ *from each* for block corners.

White fabric:
· Cut 14 strips 2½″ × width of fabric; subcut into 36 rectangles 2½″ × 4½″ and 36 rectangles 2½″ × 8½″ for blocks.
· Cut 4 strips 2″ × width of fabric; subcut into 2 strips 2″ × 36½″ and 2 strips 2″ × 39½″ for inner border.

Border fabric:
· Cut 3 strips 3¼″ × width of fabric for outer border.
· Cut 2 strips 3¼″ × 39½″ for outer border.

Binding fabric:
· Cut 5 strips 2¼″ × width of fabric.

Block Assembly

Refer to The Basics (pages 70–77) as needed. Seam allowances are ¼″ unless otherwise noted.

1. Sew a 2½″ × 4½″ white rectangle to opposite sides of a 4½″ × 4½″ print square. Press the seams toward the white fabric.

2. Sew a 2½″ × 2½″ print square to both ends of a 2½″ × 4½″ white rectangle. Press the seams toward the white fabric. Make 2.

3. Sew the units from Step 2 to the top and bottom of the unit from Step 1. Press the seams away from the center.

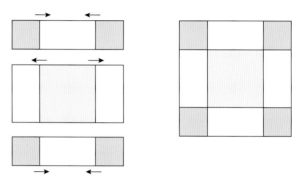

4. Sew a 2½″ × 8½″ white rectangle to opposite sides of the unit from Step 3. Press the seams toward the white fabric.

5. Sew a 2½″ × 2½″ print square to both sides of a 2½″ × 8½″ white rectangle. Make 2. Press toward the white fabric.

6. Sew the units from Step 5 to the top and bottom of the units from Step 4. Repeat Steps 1–6 to make 9 blocks.

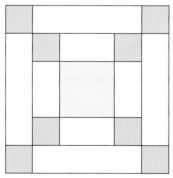

Make 9.

Quilt Assembly

1. Arrange and sew the blocks into 3 rows of 3 blocks each. Press the seams in opposite direction from row to row. Sew the rows together. Press the seams in one direction.

2. Sew the 2″ × 36½″ white borders to the sides of the quilt. Press the seams toward the borders. Sew the 2″ × 39½″ white borders to the top and bottom of quilt. Press.

3. Sew the 3¼″ × 39½″ print borders to the sides of quilt. Press the seams toward the outer borders.

4. Sew 3 print 3¼″ × 42″ border strips together and cut into 2 pieces 3¼″ × 45″ for the top and bottom of the quilt. Sew to the quilt and press the seams toward the outer borders.

5. Layer the backing, batting, and quilt top. Quilt as desired. Bind the edges (see Binding, pages 76 and 77).

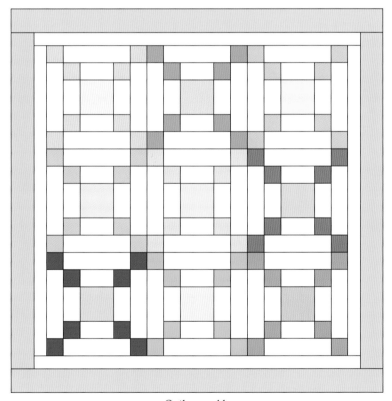

Quilt assembly

Organizing Scraps

Almost every quilter will agree that organizing scraps is an ongoing challenge. Over the past few years I've really been inspired to save my scraps and to organize them for easy use. It's always fulfilling to make a quilt completely from scraps! I gather ideas for scrap organization whenever I can. Below are a few of my favorite ideas.

I know that many of my great-great-grandmother's quilts were made using carefully saved scraps, and it is a lot of fun to repeat that history. I love seeing modern-day scrap quilts!

- If I know I have enough coordinating scraps for a table runner or a few potholders, I keep them in a plastic zipper bag with a note on the outside of the bag listing some ideas for their use. When I need to make something fast, I'll go through my collection of coordinated scrap bags and choose one to sew with.

- Organizing scraps in separate boxes or bins by color is probably the most preferred way to organize extra pieces. (It's a lot of fun to just rummage through them too.) In the past I've used plastic shoeboxes for this, but because I often smell a plastic odor when opening boxes that haven't been used in a while, I'm in the process of moving my scraps to open-air wire bins.

- Another useful idea is to cut up extra fabrics at the end of a project into commonly used sizes. I have a few bins of 2½″-wide strips, a bin of 1½″-wide strips, a box of 5″ × 5″ squares, as well as boxes of 2½″ × 2½″ and 3″ × 3″ squares. I've also recently started a half-square triangle box for a half-square triangle scrap quilt to be made someday!

Quilt Labels

Close-up of the Dresden quilt pieced by Emma Acelia Wakefield Fitzgarrald
and assembled and hand quilted by Jean Bice Bontrager Wilkins

Recording information about your quilts is an important part of quiltmaking. The journal notes I have from one of my great-great-grandmothers about her quilts are absolutely priceless. I appreciate being able to read her everyday thoughts about making quilts in the 1930s, 1940s, and 1950s.

I tried unsuccessfully for many years to document my quiltmaking projects; I ultimately began my blog in an effort to finally have a record of my projects. Blogging turned out to be the best way for me to keep track of everything. Of course, different methods work better for different quilters, and you might find that recording notes in a journal or scrapbook works best for you. Whichever method you choose, you'll be grateful for your records.

Labeling your quilts is an important way to document your creative projects. Some things you might want to include in a quilt label are your name, the quilter's name (if someone else did this), the name of the quilt, the pattern name, fabric information, where the quilt was made, and the dates when the quilt was started and completed. Some quilters have a lot of fun adding quotations or extra information about the quilt to their labels.

Grandma's Garden quilt label (I renamed this quilt for the book.)

Parlor quilt label

Newport quilt label

Labels can be as simple as a premade twill tag with your name printed on it. They can be printed using a computer, inkjet printer, and fabric that has been prepared for inkjet printing or fabric backed with freezer paper. Another method of making labels involves using an archival pen to record the information. My grandmother created elaborate embroidered labels for some of her favorite quilts. I've used each of these methods and prefer either handwriting or printing the information by computer onto fabric, which I then appliqué to the back of the quilt. Quilt labels can even be sewn into a strip on the backing of the quilt before quilting to ensure that they are always part of the quilt.

Some of the labels made for the quilts in this book were made using *Quilt Label Collective, Volume 1*, a CD with line art made especially for quilt labels published by C&T Publishing.

The Basics

Photo by Korindi Olson Totten

Fabric Selection

Fabric selection is something that most quilters want to make sure they "get right." As a new quilter I was intimidated by choosing colors and fabrics. I often relied on my grandmother and aunt to help me choose fabrics; it always seemed they had a better eye for color than I did. As I quilted more and more, I began to develop a little more confidence in my color choices.

Here's one piece of advice I received from quilter Carrie Nelson that might be helpful to others: Make note of what you like in other quilts that you see. Record your thoughts about colors and fabrics in a quiltmaking journal. Are you always drawn to a particular type of quilt? Make note of that. Pay attention to how much open space you like in the quilts you see. Do you like a little white in your quilts, or do you like a lot of white? What about creams—are you more drawn to them? What colors appeal to you again and again? By keeping track of your likes and dislikes in other quilts, you'll be able to get a better idea of what fabrics you'll love the most. Then, sew with what you love. Sometimes small projects like table runners and pillows can be a great way to test your fabric selections before using them in a larger quilt.

Inspiration Boards

One quiltmaking tool that has been an invaluable resource is what I call my inspiration board. I made mine using a large frame from an old mirror. I spray painted the frame and then wrapped the laminate backing board with two layers of batting. I used a staple gun to attach the board to the frame. This hangs on the wall in my sewing room. Fabric and blocks cling to the batting so I can I put pieces of fabric on the board, as well as sample quilt blocks that I'm working on. I have one of my great-great-grandmother's quilt blocks on it as well.

Large inspiration board

I also have a small pushpin bulletin board in my sewing room that I use to pin photos and magazine clippings that inspire me. I also pin up quotations that I like and little snips of fabric.

Small inspiration board

Inspiration boards

71

Supplies and Tools

Every quilter needs a few basic items:

- Pair of sharp scissors: I prefer a lightweight pair.

- Rotary cutter

- Self-healing cutting mat

- Acrylic rulers: I find that I most often use the 6″ × 12″ and 8″ × 24″ rulers in my collection.

- Sharp seam ripper: Although we can always hope that we don't need one, it seems I use mine fairly frequently.

- Glass-head pins and pincushion: It's much handier to store and use pins when you can easily take them in and out of a pincushion.

- Iron

- Fine-lead mechanical pencil: I use this to mark lines when needed for half-square triangles and corner triangle units.

- Sharpie or other permanent marker for making freezer-paper templates

Of course, there are endless options for other gadgets, and I can honestly say I haven't met a specialty tool or ruler that I didn't love!

Cutting

One of the first things my grandmother taught me about making quilts involved an old adage that you may be familiar with: Measure twice and cut once. I remember repeating that in my mind when I first started quiltmaking—I didn't want to waste any of the precious fabric I was working with. Even now, when I make a cutting error, it's usually because I didn't double-check my measurements.

Regarding cutting technique, I follow two rules.

- Rule Number One: Always cut with a sharp rotary cutting blade.

- Rule Number Two: Square up your fabric before you begin to cut. Line up the bottom edge of your fabric with one of the lines on your cutting mat. Then make an even cut along the left edge of the fabric, lining up the ruler with lines on the mat at the top and bottom. Occasionally repeat the squaring up of your fabric, especially if you are cutting several strips or pieces from one piece of fabric.

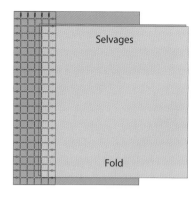

The ¼″ Seam

An accurate ¼″ seam is essential for piecing. I have to admit that I pieced for several years before I learned a handy way to check if my ¼″ seam was measuring up.

1. Sew a ¼″ seam using the method you would normally use.

2. Measure your seam allowance with an acrylic ruler to see the real measurement. It should be a thread's width narrower than ¼″ to allow for space taken up by the seam allowance when pressing.

If your seam is too wide or too narrow, see if you can move your needle a little to the right or left to solve the problem. You can also make a seam guide: place an acrylic ruler under your presser foot, aligning the needle just a scant bit to the right of the ¼″ mark (the majority of the ruler will be to the left of the presser foot). Using a few pieces of painter's tape, build up a guide with an edge to place your fabric against as you sew. This will create a perfect ¼″ seam every time, and the painter's tape is easy to remove. Most makes of machines also have a special ¼″ foot available; however, it is important to measure your seam to make sure it is on target, even when using a ¼″ foot.

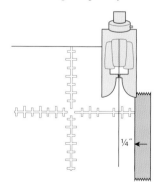

Making a seam guide

Half-Square Triangles

To make half-square triangle units, place 2 squares of fabric right sides together. Draw a diagonal line from corner to corner on the wrong side of the top square (usually the lighter fabric). Sew ¼˝ away from each side of the drawn line; then cut on the drawn line. You will have 2 identical half-square triangle units. Press the seams open and trim. The specific sizes of the squares are provided in the instructions where this technique is used.

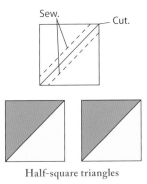

Half-square triangles

My Favorite Ruler

The Fit to Be Quarter ruler is especially helpful in trimming half-square triangle units. This ruler is the absolute best ruler I've found for trimming half-square triangles, quarter-square triangles, and combination units. It is also very helpful for simply squaring up quilt blocks. One of the best things about this ruler is that it can be used for blocks ranging in size from ½˝ to 9˝. (See Resources, page 78.)

Corner-Square Triangles

To make corner-square triangles (as used in the Snowball blocks and Flying Geese), draw a diagonal line from corner to corner on the wrong side of the smaller square. Place the smaller square on top of the larger square or rectangle, right sides together, making sure the sides of the squares are aligned. Sew on the drawn line. Trim the seam allowance to ¼″ and press the seam toward the corner. The specific sizes of the squares and/or rectangles are provided in the project instructions where this technique is used.

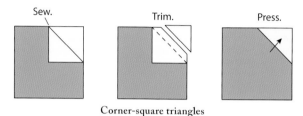

Corner-square triangles

Making Freezer-Paper Templates

1. Trace the pattern onto the shiny side of freezer paper using a Sharpie or other permanent marker.

2. Cut out the shape ½″ outside of the drawn line. Place the shiny side of the cutout shape on the dull side of another piece of freezer paper and press the 2 pieces together. Cut out the shape on the drawn line. You will now have a double-layered freezer-paper template that can be ironed to your fabric.

3. When ironing, make sure the shiny side of the template is against the wrong side of the fabric. Cut out the fabric ¼″ to ⅜″ outside the edges of the template.

Appliqué Basics

Appliqué can be done by machine, but I prefer to hand appliqué most of my work. Prepare the appliqué piece as directed in the project, turning the seam allowance under and pressing or basting it before positioning it on the background.

1. Place and secure the piece to be appliquéd on top of the background fabric. Short appliqué pins may be used to secure your work, or you can use specially made water-soluble glues. With glue, place a small dot of glue every ½″ or so on the back of the appliqué piece, taking care to ensure that the glue is away from the very edge of the fabric where you will be stitching. Roxanne Glue-Baste-It and Jill Finley's Appli-Glue are good basting glues. When using pins, Clover appliqué pins are sharp and easy to work with, yet small enough to not get in the way.

2. Use a neutral-colored silk thread or a silk-finish cotton thread in a color that matches the piece to be appliquéd. Thread a needle and knot the thread.

3. Come up from the wrong side of the background fabric through the fabric to be appliquéd, very close to the turned-under edge where the appliqué piece meets the background fabric.

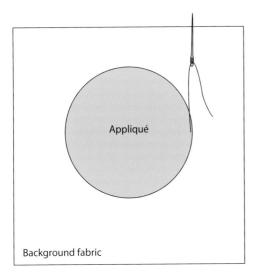

4. Take the needle and thread straight down into the background fabric right next to where your needle came up and close to the edge of the appliqué.

5. Slide the needle about ⅛″ counterclockwise and come up again, bringing the needle and thread through the appliqué piece and catching just a few threads along the edge of the appliqué.

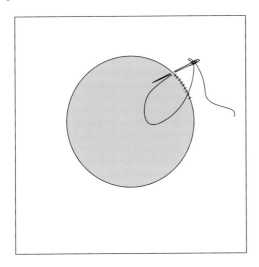

6. Repeat this stitch all around the appliqué piece until it is secured to the background fabric.

All traveling stitches will be on the back of the fabric where they won't show, leaving just tiny stitches on the front of your work.

Borders

Wait until the quilt top is complete to cut the border strips. Always measure the length and width of your quilt through the center and compare the actual measurements of your quilt with the measurements given in the pattern. Pattern measurements are mathematical calculations based on an exact ¼″ seam and don't take into account any stretching, bias, or differences in seam allowances.

If the borders are longer than 40″ or 42″, sew the border strips into one long piece before cutting them to fit. This way, the seams will end up in different places on the quilt, helping to make them less noticeable.

1. Place 2 strips together at a 90° angle, right sides together. Draw a diagonal line from the top left corner of the top strip to the bottom right corner of the bottom strip. Sew on this line. Trim the seam allowance to ¼″. I press the seams open to reduce bulk.

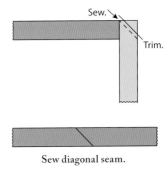

Sew diagonal seam.

2. Always pin the border pieces to the quilt top, easing as necessary to ensure that everything still matches up when you get to the end of the seam. Pin at each end, in the center, and at the midpoints between the center and ends. Generally, the side borders are sewn first and then the top and bottom.

3. Repeat Steps 1 and 2 for any additional borders.

Backing

Unless you purchase extra-wide fabric for your quilt backings, most backings will need to be pieced. Seams may be pieced vertically or horizontally to make best use of the fabric. Scrappy backs are a lot of fun to make. Making a scrappy back is a good way to use up extra fabrics from the front of your quilt. Whether you use a single fabric or several different pieces, be sure that the backing measures 3″ to 6″ larger in each direction than your quilt top. Smaller quilts need less extra fabric than larger ones.

Binding

I nearly always use a double-fold binding that I stitch by machine to the right side of the quilt, and then fold over and stitch in place by hand to the back side of the quilt.

I usually cut binding strips at 2¼″ or 2½″. Occasionally I will use 2″ strips if I want a very narrow edge. To prepare binding, sew all the strips together using a diagonal seam as for piecing borders (page 75). Press the strip in half with wrong sides together, aligning the long raw edges. Sew to your quilt top as directed in Applying Binding (page 77).

I always press the binding outward and then use binding clips to keep it secure while I do the hand stitching.

Scrappy Binding

Scrappy bindings are a lot of fun to make, and they are the perfect solution if you forgot to buy binding fabric when you purchased the fabric for your quilt. *Grandma's Garden* (page 42) is made with a scrappy binding using leftover red Jelly Roll strips from the quilt top.

For a scrappy binding I cut strips 2½″ × width of fabric and then cut these strips into four or five shorter lengths. I join strips on the diagonal until I have enough length for the binding. Sometimes I will use scraps of one color as I did in *Grandma's Garden*, but at other times I've completely mixed up the colors.

I save the leftover binding pieces from all of my quilts in a storage box, and every so often I will go through the box and sew pieces together that coordinate. More than once my bindings created from leftovers have been the perfect solution. Scrappy bindings are also fun to use with potholders and pillows.

Applying Binding

1. With raw edges even, pin the binding to the front edge of the quilt several inches away from a corner. Start sewing, using a ¼″ seam allowance, and leave the first few inches of the binding unattached.

2. Stop ¼″ away from the first corner and backstitch one stitch. Lift the presser foot and needle. Rotate the quilt one-quarter turn.

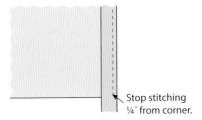

Stop stitching
¼″ from corner.

3. Fold the binding up at a right angle so it extends straight above the quilt and the fold forms a 45° angle in the corner.

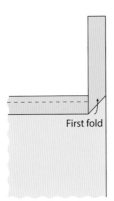

First fold

4. Fold the binding strip down, even with the next edge of the quilt. Begin sewing at the folded edge. Repeat in the same manner at all corners.

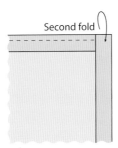

Second fold

5. Continue stitching until you are back near the beginning of the binding strip. Fold under the beginning tail of the binding strip ¼″ so that the raw edge will be inside the binding after it is turned to the back of the quilt.

6. Place the end tail of the binding strip over the beginning folded end. Continue to attach the binding and stitch slightly beyond the starting stitches. Trim the excess binding. Fold the binding over the raw edges to the quilt back and hand stitch, mitering the corners.

Staying Organized

Making quilts and creating them for your home and for those around you is an amazing hobby. It's a wonderfully creative outlet that also leaves you with treasures to adorn your home and the homes of those you know and love. So how do you keep up with all the works in progress that might be going on at any time? I have tried a variety of methods over the years and have finally found one that seems to be working extremely well!

I try to spend at least an hour once a week on planning and organizing. For me, this works best on either Friday evenings or Saturday mornings. In addition, I focus on something different each weekend.

On the first weekend of the month I get organized—make lists of things I need to accomplish for the month, go over old lists, and sometimes completely change my mind!

On the second weekend of the month I work on those notorious works in progress that everyone seems to have.

The third weekend of the month is dedicated to scraps—sometimes I'll work on organizing my scraps, and other times I'll actually sew a few blocks or a small project using them.

The fourth weekend of the month is the weekend I work on gifts for others. I'm trying to work on at least one Christmas gift a month so that I don't have to do all of my Christmas sewing at the end of the year!

Finally, when there is a fifth Friday or Saturday, I like to catch up on label making. I have several quilts from years past (made before I was very meticulous about labeling) that I'm slowly but surely getting labeled.

This system has really been working well—even if I don't get everything caught up at once, my steady progress is definitely beginning to pay off!

Resources

Supplies and Notions

Appli-Glue by Jill Finley   www.jillilystudio.com

ByAnnie's Soft and Stable   www.byannie.com

Clover Appliqué Pins   www.clover-usa.com

Dritz Cover Button Kit   www.dritz.com

Easy Dresden tool by Darlene Zimmerman   www.ezquilt.com

Fit to Be Quarter ruler by Monique Dillard   www.opengatequilts.com

Karen Kay Buckley's Perfect Circles   www.karenkaybuckley.com

Paper Pieces   www.paperpieces.com

Quilt Label Collective, Volume 1, CD published by C&T Publishing   www.ctpub.com

Marti Michell Perfect Patchwork Templates   www.frommarti.com

Roxanne Glue-Baste-It   www.colonialneedle.com

Shape-Flex   Local quilt shops or www.ctpub.com

Fabrics

The fabrics used in the quilts and projects in this book were produced by the following manufacturers:

Free Spirit   www.freespiritfabric.com

Henry Glass & Co.   www.henryglassfabrics.com

Michael Miller   www.michaelmillerfabrics.com

Moda   www.unitednotions.com

Riley Blake   www.rileyblakedesigns.com

Robert Kaufman   www.robertkaufman.com

Westminster Fibers, Inc.   www.westminsterfabrics.com